WALKING COUNTRY

TRA

A 100 mile walk across the Pennines,
from the Forest of Bowland to Fountains Abbey

HILLSIDE GUIDES - ACROSS THE NORTH

Long Distance Walks

•COAST TO COAST WALK •DALES WAY •CLEVELAND WAY
•WESTMORLAND WAY •FURNESS WAY •CUMBERLAND WAY
•LADY ANNE'S WAY •PENDLE WAY •NIDDERDALE WAY
•TRANS-PENNINE WAY •NORTH BOWLAND TRAVERSE

Hillwalking - Lake District

•LAKELAND FELLS - SOUTH •LAKELAND FELLS - EAST
•LAKELAND FELLS - NORTH •LAKELAND FELLS - WEST

Circular Walks - Peak District

•NORTHERN PEAK •EASTERN PEAK •CENTRAL PEAK
• SOUTHERN PEAK •WESTERN PEAK

Circular Walks - Yorkshire Dales

•HOWGILL FELLS •THREE PEAKS •MALHAMDALE
•WHARFEDALE •NIDDERDALE •WENSLEYDALE •SWALEDALE
•FREEDOM OF THE DALES (Large format colour hardback)

Circular Walks - North York Moors

•WESTERN MOORS •SOUTHERN MOORS •NORTHERN MOORS

Circular Walks - South Pennines

•BRONTE COUNTRY •ILKLEY MOOR
•CALDERDALE •SOUTHERN PENNINES

Circular Walks - Lancashire

•BOWLAND •PENDLE & THE RIBBLE •WEST PENNINE MOORS

Circular Walks - North Pennines

•TEESDALE •EDEN VALLEY

Yorkshire Pub Walks

•HARROGATE/WHARFE VALLEY •HAWORTH/AIRE VALLEY

Biking Guides

•YORKSHIRE DALES CYCLE WAY •WEST YORKSHIRE CYCLE WAY
•MOUNTAIN BIKING - WEST & SOUTH YORKSHIRE
•AIRE VALLEY BIKING GUIDE •CALDERDALE BIKING GUIDE
•GLASGOW Clyde Valley & Loch Lomond

•YORK WALKS *City Theme Walks*

Send for a detailed current catalogue and pricelist

WALKING COUNTRY

TRANS-PENNINE WAY

A 100 mile walk across the Pennines,
from the Forest of Bowland to Fountains Abbey

Paul Hannon

HILLSIDE

HILLSIDE
PUBLICATIONS
11 Nessfield Grove
Keighley
West Yorkshire
BD22 6NU

First published 1999

ISBN 1 870141 66 0

Whilst the author has walked and researched the entire route for the purposes of this guide, no responsibility can be accepted for any unforeseen circumstances encountered while following it. The publisher would, however, greatly appreciate any information regarding material changes, and any problems encountered.

Cover illustrations: Earl Crag, Cowling;
Parlick from Bleasdale, Forest of Bowland
Back cover: Long Bridge, in the Worth Valley
(Paul Hannon/Big Country Picture Library)

Page One: Fountains Abbey
Page Three: The Idol, Brimham Rocks

Printed in Great Britain by
Carnmor Print and Design
95-97 London Road
Preston
Lancashire
PR1 4BA

CONTENTS

White Wells, Ilkley Moor

INTRODUCTION

The Trans-Pennine Way is a 100 mile long-distance route linking Lancashire and Yorkshire, devised and first walked in 1998. Its simple aim is to traverse the full breadth of the Pennines, and while the mighty Pennine Way takes an obvious and hugely inspiring course along the backbone of England, the Trans-Pennine Way lives up to its name by offering a route linking the western and eastern extremities of Pennine country. A glance at the map reveals the western limits of Bowland and the eastern slopes of Nidderdale as prime candidates, and so an east-west crossing of 100 miles presents itself. Most folk with limited holiday time should be able to enjoy this walk in a week's duration.

Having defined the termini, the route between them literally jumps off the map, a mouth-watering roll-call of villages and fells, moors and dales: Beacon Fell, Chipping, Longridge Fell, the River Ribble, Pendle Hill, Pinhaw Beacon, Haworth, Ilkley Moor, Pateley Bridge, Brimham Rocks and Fountains Abbey. Truly a sumptuous feast, and a hundred more gems are to be found in between! The first thing to be aware of is that just because we're crossing the Pennines rather than following them, don't be misled into thinking only the middle day will take you over the hills! However, while each stage has its share of ups and downs, the walk is graded to ensure there are few major climbs, indeed the highest point of the Way barely scrapes the 1500ft contour.

Intentionally, not a single step of this superb walk ventures within a National Park, proving that you don't need to join the rush to 'Premier League' landscapes to enjoy wonderful walking. At almost every stage there are views into the Yorkshire Dales, but we never set foot within its 'official' bounds. On the subject of 'official' status, the TPW is, of course, very much an unofficial route: it has no designation as a National Trail, nor has it been created or managed by any local authorities. It is simply a pioneering walk through some of Northern England's finest scenery on legally permitted paths. Happily, however, you should find no problems other than the odd stubborn gate, or perhaps in high summer some over-enthusiastic undergrowth.

Not all designations are avoided, and the Way enjoys two Areas of Outstanding Natural Beauty (Forest of Bowland and Nidderdale), as well as the South Pennines Heritage Area. It also follows short sections of other named routes, not through lack of imagination, but simply because their numbers are such that they cannot all be skirted.

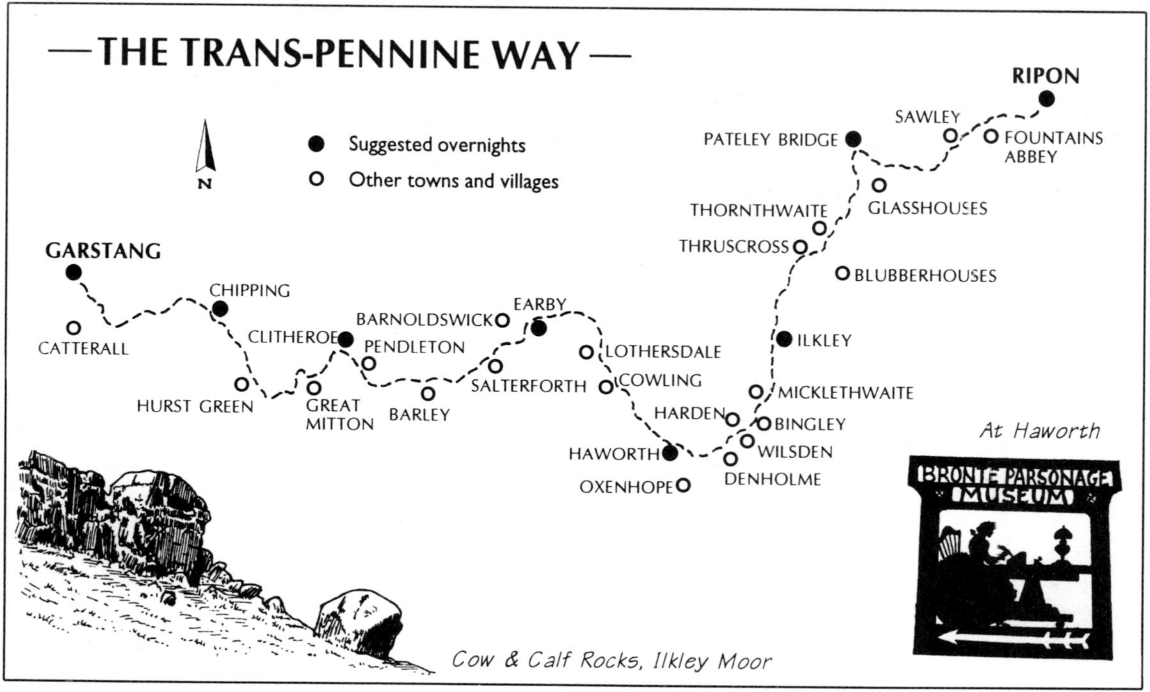

Cow & Calf Rocks, Ilkley Moor

At Haworth

Both the route's termini are well served by buses, Garstang from Preston and Lancaster, and Ripon from Harrogate. All three of these have good onward rail services. Public transport linking the daily stages is mentioned at the start of each chapter. Several interesting diversions highlighted in the text offer scope for varying the route. The most appealing is an alternative route through the Fountains Abbey & Studley Royal estate. Because this involves an entry fee it has not been deemed the main route, but few will turn down the chance to savour such a magnificent landscape.

Although the route has been checked with local authorities, be mindful that paths can change, so please adhere to any official diversions. Be kind to the countryside you pass through, leaving only footprints and taking only photographs. Walking is the greenest form of travel, and the only way to really explore places. Most people will enjoy many new sights during this walk, and will hopefully be tempted back to become better acquainted with some of these areas.

Using the guide

The guide divides into seven stages, each giving a comfortable day's walk and ending at a suitable place (an accommodation list is freely available from the publisher on receipt of a S.A.E.), though numerous permutations can be made. Each stage is self-contained, essential information being followed by a simple map and a concise route description. Dovetailed between are notes of features along the way, and interspersed are illustrations which capture the flavour of the walk. Essential route description has been highlighted in bold, making it easily accessible amongst the other snippets of information. The sketch maps serve only to identify the location of the route, and whilst the description should be sufficient to guide one around, a 1:25,000 scale Ordnance Survey map is recommended. The following cover the route (these are also mentioned at the start of each chapter):

•*Outdoor Leisure 21 - South Pennines*
•*Outdoor Leisure 41 - Forest of Bowland & Ribblesdale*
•*Pathfinder 682 - Bradford (to be replaced by Explorer map in 2000)*
•*Explorer 19 - West Pennine Moors*
•*Explorer 26 - Nidderdale*
•*Explorer 27 - Lower Wharfedale & Washburn Valley*
(the Explorer maps are to be re-numbered at some point)

Additionally, these 1:50,000 Landranger maps cover the route:

102 - Preston & Blackpool
103 - Blackburn & Burnley
104 - Leeds, Bradford & Harrogate
99 - Northallerton & Ripon

SOME USEFUL FACILITIES - *A general guide only*

	YH/camping barn	Accommodation	Camping	Bus service	Rail station	Pub	Post office	Other shop	WC	Phone	Cafe
Garstang		●	●	●		●	●	●	●	●	●
Canal (end)		●				●					
Claughton										●	
Beacon Fell				●					●		●
Bleasdale							●				●
Chipping	●	●		●		●	●	●	●	●	●
Gibbon Bridge		●		●		●					
Walker Fold		●		●		●				●	
Hurst Green	●	●		●		●	●		●	●	
Great Mitton		●		●		●				●	●
Clitheroe		●	●	●	●	●	●	●	●	●	●
Pendleton				●		●				●	
Nick of Pendle				●		●					
Sabden				●		●	●	●	●	●	●
Barley		●		●		●			●	●	●
Roughlee		●		●		●				●	
A682, Admergill		●	●			●					
Salterforth		●	●	●		●	●		●	●	
Barnoldswick		●		●		●	●	●	●	●	●
Earby	●	●		●		●	●	●	●	●	●
Lothersdale		●	●			●				●	
Cowling		●	●	●		●	●	●	●	●	
Oldfield		●				●				●	
Haworth	●	●	●	●	●	●	●	●	●	●	●
Oxenhope		●	●	●	●	●	●	●	●	●	●
Denholme		●		●		●	●	●	●	●	
Cullingworth		●		●		●	●	●	●	●	●
Harden				●		●	●	●	●	●	
Wilsden				●		●	●	●		●	●
Bingley		●		●	●	●	●	●	●	●	●
Crossflatts				●	●	●	●	●	●	●	●
Micklethwaite										●	
Ilkley		●	●	●	●	●	●	●	●	●	●
Thruscross						●					
Thornthwaite										●	
Bewerley		●								●	
Pateley Bridge		●	●	●		●	●	●	●	●	●
Glasshouses				●		●	●		●	●	●
Brimham Rocks		●		●				●	●		●
Sawley			●			●				●	
Fountains Abbey		●		●				●	●		●
Studley Roger		●								●	
Ripon		●	●	●		●	●	●	●	●	●

STAGE 1

GARSTANG TO CHIPPING

Distance: 12 miles/19km

Map:
1:50,000
Landranger 102 - Preston & Blackpool
1:25,000
Outdoor Leisure 41 - Forest of Bowland & Ribblesdale

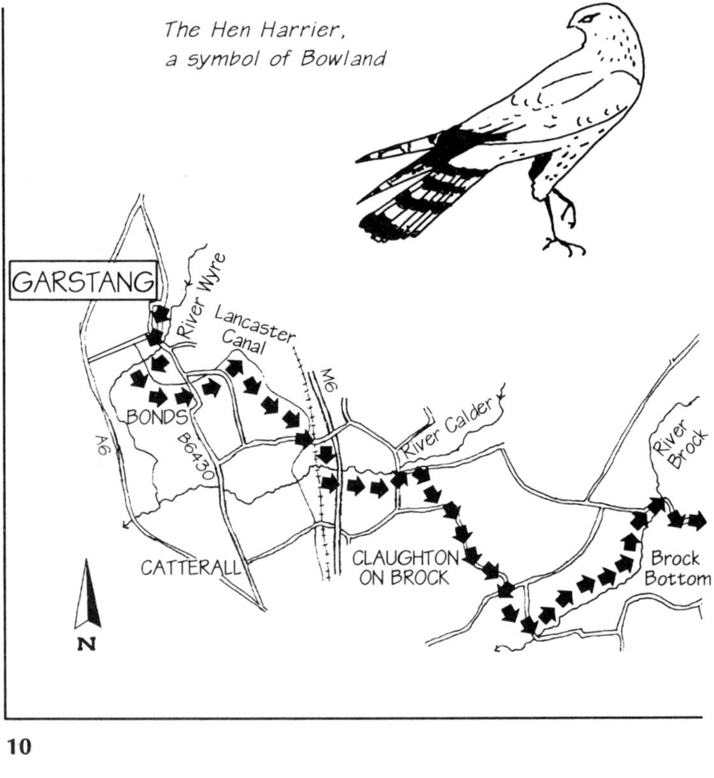

The opening stage begins on river and canal banks that curve beneath the westernmost Pennine slopes, the heathery Bleasdale Moors being within a stone's throw high above. Rural idyll and the wooded river Brock lead to the miniature eminence of Beacon Fell, a perfect grandstand for delectable Bowland country. On the lower slopes of shapely Parlick there is an option to visit its windswept summit before descending to the cosy village of Chipping.

•*Transport links: Garstang is on the regular Preston-Lancaster bus route, and is also served from Blackpool. There are direct bus services from Chipping to both Longridge (for Preston) and Clitheroe.*

Brabin's School, Chipping

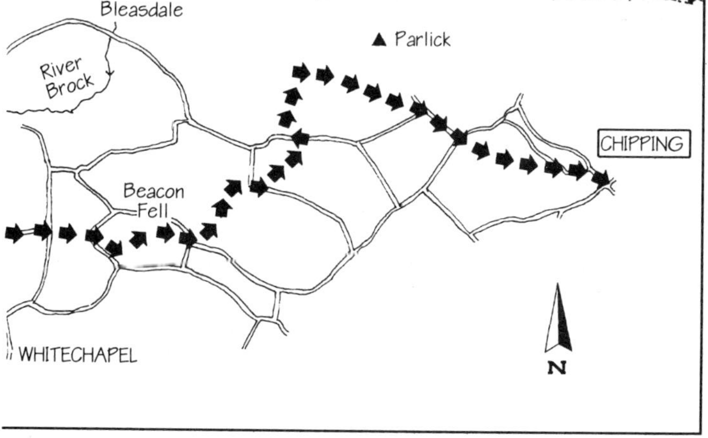

• *GARSTANG*

The town of Garstang stands on the western bank of the river Wyre, with the Lancaster Canal neatly closing in from the other side. Garstang is capital of the eastern, rural half of the Wyre district, and also sits at the very western extremity of the Pennines. Within a mile of here, immediately across the M6, farmed slopes rise onto the Bowland moors. Indeed, the Forest of Bowland AONB boundary comes within two miles of the town.

The little town once had its own railway station, not on the main line, however, but on a local branch line (the 'Pilling Pig') that ran to Knott End-on-Sea, at the Wyre's estuary. Today the West Coast Main Line whizzes past from Preston to Lancaster, within a mile of Garstang but not slowing down to acknowledge it. A more recent transport artery the M6 motorway does likewise, and it is odd that this major settlement between Preston and Lancaster is not afforded its own junction: good grief, Shap's got one!

Focal point for visitors is the Discovery Centre, with displays of local history and wildlife as well as tourist information. Facing it across the High Street is the Old Grammar School, founded in 1756: it closed as a school in 1928 and currently houses an arts centre. Garstang's busy day is Thursday, when the market straggles along the length of the High Street. Here the Market House and the old Town Hall stand side by side, and close by is the market cross. This recalls the restoration of the market in 1680, though the town had gained its first such charter as far back as 1310. A number of narrow alleys - 'wiends' - radiate from the High Street, while stood further back is the parish church of St. Thomas.

The Wyre Aqueduct, Garstang

➡ **Start from the 'Riverside Trail' information board on a large bend of the riverbank. This is reached by crossing the car park from the Wyre Discovery Centre at the northern end of the High Street.** This lovely spot offers a glimpse of the Bleasdale Moors on the horizon. **Turn right, downstream on an urbanised path which accompanies the Wyre for a short but pleasant start.** The river Wyre is the first of a handful we are to encounter that begin life as lively streams racing off the Bowland moors. It is formed by the merging of the Tarnbrook Wyre and the Marshaw Wyre at Abbeystead, beneath Ward's Stone, the highest point in Bowland. Arrival at Garstang marks its farewell to the hill country, and a contrastingly flat journey leads to a sizeable estuary at Fleetwood.

Before reaching Garstang Bridge we are forced away from the river along Coach House Mews, to join Bridge Street at the bottom end of the High Street. Turn left to cross the bridge, and immediately over it turn right along a short driveway. Pass under the archway at this former cornmill, now a nursing home. At the end of the car park a grassy path runs into trees, and the river returns for company as a large stone bridge is reached. This is the single span Garstang Aqueduct, which carries the Lancaster Canal over the Wyre. Completed in 1797 by the renowned engineer John Rennie, it stands 34ft high and 110ft long. **Underneath it the footpath ends, so turn up some wooden steps to gain the canal towpath.** Along to the left is the colourful scene at a wide basin, where also stands *Th'Owd Tithebarn*, now converted into a popular pub almost resembling a museum.

The route however turns right, to trace the canal towpath for the next mile and a half. This leisurely start makes a fine introduction to the route, and a charming corridor out of town. **Three stone arched road bridges are passed under before the modern suburbs of Bonds, across the water, are left behind. Now in truly open country, the first feature of note is the ruin of Greenhalgh Castle on its prominent knoll over to the left.** Built in 1490 by Thomas Stanley, Earl of Derby, it was attacked by Parliamentarian forces during the Civil War who ultimately left it as the shell we see today. Additionally, the view ahead is enhanced by the heathery skyline of Bleasdale Moors.

The Lancaster Canal was officially opened in 1797 for 43 miles between Preston and Tewitfield, though it was not until 1819 that its northern extremity was reached at Kendal. The canal also extended south to Wigan. Its main role was the carriage of goods such as quarried lime southwards, for agriculture, and coal northwards, for industry. By the 1860s the far more efficient railways had already decimated the waterway's viability, and a long decline began. Indeed, the final miles to Kendal have long since been drained, though the Lancaster Canal Trust, which seeks to conserve the canal for all users, has a long-term aim of seeing it restored all the way back to Kendal.

The canal makes a large loop to the right, passing beneath three further bridges in farming surrounds. Much of the ensuing way is on a delectable green towpath in far better condition than my lawn. The canal is left at Ray Lane, the next road bridge (number 54). Double back up steps onto the road and cross the canal, immediately followed by passing beneath the railway. On the left the *Kenlis Arms* offers a refreshment halt for those making a late start.

The way turns sharp right at this road junction, through a gate into a field to follow a track parallel to the railway embankment. Across an iron bridge on the river Calder, a tall motorway footbridge awaits to the left. Advance a little further then cross the field to it. From this relatively airy vantage point a clear day earns surprisingly extensive views. Westwards across the Fylde rises Blackpool Tower, but keen eyes will be drawn north-west to a wide sweep of Lakeland Fells.

Over the bridge, head away upstream between the winding Calder and a hedgerow. The river Calder is no more than a lively moorland beck as it carves a fast-flowing course down from Bleasdale Moors, to be absorbed by the Wyre a mile south of Garstang. **River and hedge converge to join a farm track leading out onto a road. Go left briefly to a junction at Sandholme Bridge.** Across it is the former Sandholme Mill, converted to residential use. **Don't cross the bridge but turn right up Butt Hill Lane. After a good 200 yards take a gate on the right, just before a farm on the left (and just before the power lines).**

With a hedge on the right, cross just a few yards to another gate in front, then rise left with a fence. A substantial hedge is joined and followed along to the right. From this very modest elevation there are more extensive views over the Fylde: there's nothing this flat until the eastward views at the opposite end of the Way, and even then you'll have the North York Moors skyline on a clear day. **From a corner stile continue along to a gate as the fence bends right. Now cross to the farm at Crabtree Nook just ahead, entering its yard and passing left of the house to emerge onto a back road, Smithy Lane.**

Turn left for a good stride during which the motorway drone can be escaped in pleasant rural surrounds. Almost at once a cross is passed on the left. Restored into an ancient base is a World War One memorial from William Fitzherbert Brockhouse, whose two sons are remembered along with local people. **Passing Cross House Farm with its attractive pond, the road runs on to the scattered hamlet of Claughton-on-Brock.** The Roman Catholic church of St. Thomas the Apostle stands in what appears an almost congregation-free zone, and its unassuming appearance belies a beautiful interior. It dates back some two centuries, and featuring prominently inside are reminders of numerous local priests who were martyred for their faith in the 16th and 17th centuries. **The road runs on past a tiny school and lovely red-brick cottages to a T-junction with May Lane.**

Walk a few yards right and turn left along a short farm drive. Level with the white-walled house, don't advance to the gate at the end, but locate a small stile in the hedge to the right. Now turn left along the fieldside to a stile in the bottom corner. The wooded valley of the river Brock nestles in front, with the bare top of Parlick to the left beyond wooded Beacon Fell. **Drop left to pass a hedge corner and down to a footbridge straddling both hedge and ditch to emerge onto another back road. Turn down this to quickly arrive at Walmsley Bridge on the river Brock.**

From a kissing-gate on the left turn upstream, an intermittent path crossing a pasture to briefly enter riverside woodland. The river Brock has a near-identical life to the Calder, enjoying the same moorland birth and again submitting to the Wyre, just a couple of miles beyond the Calder's demise. **Re-emerging, continue upstream for some time, the tree-lined Brock being matched by a wooded bank to the left. On approaching a tall hedge coming down from the left in this otherwise open pasture, bear left with it, crossing a sidestream and slanting up to the field top, where a gate and kissing-gate admit onto an old cart track. Turn right on this, dropping down to run on through well wooded surrounds.**

Part way on, a guidepost sends a permissive path running to the right for 100 yards to find the scant remains of a mill. The first building here was a late 18th century paper mill, and having been resurrected for various uses the site was last worked in the 1920s. This was one of four mills served by the Brock: all are now gone, long having succumbed to the steam powered mills that appeared on the plain below.

The main path continues on, pleasantly if sometimes muddily, to quickly arrive at a footbridge across the river at Brock Bottom. This overgrown area is the site of some former millworkers' cottages. **Don't cross the bridge but resume upstream on what has been dubbed the Brock Valley Nature Trail.** Through undergrowth, initially, the bank is soon rejoined at a long collapsed weir. **This smashing path runs up through superb wooded surrounds to the Brock car park and picnic area at Higher Brock Bridge.**

Higher Brock Bridge

Cross the bridge and leave the river on the road (White Lee Lane) climbing steeply away. It eases out and rises gently through a veritable avenue of trees to a T-junction. Towards the top, little iron gates on either side indicate the course of the Thirlmere Aqueduct carrying Manchester's drinking water from the Lake District. By the junction, Bowland's fells have become appreciably clearer just across to the left, usurping the modest knoll of Beacon Fell directly in front. **Go a few yards right to a stile and cross the field to a footbridge, then resume the 'ascent' of Beacon Fell up a wooded bank. A path climbs as far as a hurdle-stile, after which continue directly up a steep field.**

A stile at the top is gained where fence and wall meet, by which time a serious break will have been earned to appraise the sweeping view westwards. Looking beyond the wooded Brock Valley to the Fylde, this vast plain still retains many trees to bound its patchwork fields. The Lakeland Fells, seen so early from the motorway bridge, are now much better arrayed beyond the waters of Morecambe Bay: Black Combe overlooks the Barrow shipyards, while further right is a fair grouping of the major fells of the Southern Lakes. **Rise to another stile just above, and through the trees the road encircling Beacon Fell is joined. Turn right to quickly arrive at the Bowland Visitor Centre.**

The Lancaster Canal at Garstang

Fair Snape Fell and Parlick across Bleasdale, from Beacon Fell

A corner of Chipping

The Bowland moors from Longridge Fell

Beacon Fell was opened in 1970 as Lancashire's first country park, comprising 185 acres of moorland and woodland. To Lancashire folk it is a much valued and well used amenity. The new visitor centre opened in 1995, and provides information, displays, a shop, refreshments and toilets. Its predecessor, Fell House Information Centre, recalled the original farmhouse demolished in 1939, some 30 years after the fell had become a gathering ground for nearby Barns Fold Reservoirs.

From the grassy area alongside the centre a well built path rises away from an information board, bearing left through trees to emerge onto the open summit of the fell. Better though to take the public footpath which starts at the same point but climbs more directly into the trees. Ignoring any other ways rise with an old wall through the trees and on to their far end, emerging with a contrastingly fine view over the inspiring cirque of Bleasdale fells. Turn right on the path rising between moor and trees to a surprisingly sudden arrival at the white-painted Ordnance Survey column.

This crowns Beacon Fell at the very modest height of 872ft/266m, yet it is nevertheless the highest point of the day. Affixed to it are a plaque and a view indicator. Some of its features are distinctly under-represented thanks to the growth of trees to south and east, though everything we want to see is readily on display. The fell gets its name from its former role, as a beacon site for perhaps 1000 years: certainly it was part of the chain that warned of the approach of the Spanish Armada in 1588.

Beacon Fell, looking to Fair Snape Fell and Parlick

Resume eastwards on the main path across the moorland, the surround of trees keeping sufficient distance to have little impact on the views. The path slants gently down to run above a parallel one on the top edge of the trees. It doesn't join it as expected, but runs on to part of the Quarry car park. Follow the little road out through heather colonised knolls to meet the fell's circuit road again. An attractive pond down to the right makes a good foreground to views south-eastwards to an array of Pennine moors.

Go left a few yards to a junction, then right on a road descending away to the east. Within yards however leave this by a stile on the left, and cross to the brow of the field before slanting right, down to a fence corner. From this field we can once again survey a magnificent prospect of Bleasdale country, backed by the great cirque of fells of Parlick and Fair Snape. Also in view to the right are Easington Fell, Pendle Hill and Longridge Fell. **At the fence corner an old hollowed way is met. Follow this left down the field-sides. As it swings right for Wood Acre, take a stile/gate in front and continue down one further field-side. At the bottom corner ignore the stile in front and turn right to approach the buildings. After an intervening stile, a stile in the fence just before it keeps us out of its confines, advancing to a gate to follow the drive out onto a road.**

Go right as far as Watery Gate Farm, past which take a gate on the left just before a line of trees. Double back left a few yards to trace a sunken pathway away with a fence. From a stile at the far end bear right over the brow, and cross towards Lower Core Farm. A gate in front admits onto another road. Go left for a couple of minutes and turn up the drive through the fields to Blindhurst. Now we're really on the slopes of Parlick, which rises invitingly above. Entering the yard at Blindhurst, note the attractive front of the white-walled house, complete with a 1731 datestone and mullioned and transomed windows.

Pass to the right of the house into an enclosure, but instead of following the track away, turn up the wallside to a fence above. Just a little beyond the gate an initially faint green way slants across the field. A guidepost here indicates the start of an optional detour onto Parlick: see panel opposite. **The green way quickly levels out and crosses to a tiny brook, beyond which slant up towards a stile onto the foot of the fell proper at an access notice.**

• *PARLICK*

If considering a detour onto Parlick, be aware in advance that the described route onto it is within the Wolf Fell Access Area, which may be closed on a number of days during the grouse shooting season (from August 12th, but not Sundays) and at times of high fire risk. Restrictions include no dogs and no fires.

The sign above Blindhurst sends a concessionary path rising directly up the field as a quickly forming, sunken green way. This climbs to a gate on to the base of the fell. Bear right on a sunken way winding up the steep slopes to enter the access area at another fence. Continuing a zigzag climb up Parlick's steep contours, a crumbled wall is approached. Now slant across to the fence on the right, soon easing out to attain the summit at 1417ft/432m.

In truth this is a rather ordinary top, but its situation is not. The panorama from the great pile of stones is outstanding. Anti-clockwise we have the West Pennine Moors, the South Pennines, Longridge Fell, Pendle Hill, Easington Fell, and round via Saddle Fell to Bleasdale Moors. Looking back, Fair Snape's west top is now looking magnificent. Parlick (Parlick Pike is its rarely used Sunday name) is a haunt of hang-gliders, and if in evidence they add a further touch of colour to the scene.

Leave by the path heading south-east to quickly encounter steep ground. Fell Foot Farm waits directly below. As Parlick is a popular objective, the path on its steep flank is becoming rather worn. On encountering a traversing path, take advantage of its easy gradients and turn down to the right on one of its sunken ways, thence doubling back to the base of the fell. This not only limits erosion, it makes a far more civilised descent. At Fell Foot the head of a lane is met. Follow this down to a junction to rejoin the main route.

Parlick's summit cairn, looking east

Parlick from Saddle Fell, to the east

Ignoring this stile, advance to another in the field corner just beyond. Cross the head of a tree-lined trickle and contour across the large field. There are sweeping views ahead to Longridge Fell. **Locate a particularly substantial stile built into the wall at the end, then angle gently down the next pasture to a stile above a few scattered trees. Resume the contour across a larger field to a ladder-stile at the far end.** By now Pendle is fully in position beyond Longridge Fell, with the sprawl of Clitheroe at its foot. In good light one can also discern the white-walled *Wellsprings Inn* under the southern slopes of the fell.

Slant down this final pasture to a stile onto the cul-de-sac road descending from Fell Foot. To the right is a junction with a through road: turn down this (left) to a T-junction with Fish House Lane. Look back to the left to see Saddle Fell and Burnslack Fell now slotting into place to the east of Parlick. A quiet road walk can be enjoyed by going left, descent past the wooded clough of Chipping Brook being entirely delightful, especially when the bluebells are in bloom.

Otherwise, cross straight over to a stile, and follow a crumbling wall away. This curves down Lingey Hill to be replaced by a few trees and a tiny beck. At the bottom of a steeper slope the old way becomes enclosed, but in practise is impassable. A fence-stile to its left sees us down the field-side outside the morass. Occasional waymarks help confirm the route, which actually takes a messy way either side of the stream. Supposedly, at a gateway in the old way (before a side-stream on the left), cross the marshy section and resume down the hedgerow side to the corner just below.

Here the stream's dark confines are entered, crossing to the other side to continue downstream again. A little further, before the corner and the barn of After Lee, superfluous stepping-stones cross the beck to an adjacent wall-stile. Rise away to a stile part-hidden by holly at a kink in the fence above. Head directly away from this - with Springs House over to the right - to a stile onto its drive. Turn left to join a back road, and follow this down to the right and into the village. En route we pass the camping barn at Clark House, first building on the right.

Chipping is an attractive stone built village, whose origins pre-date its emergence as a market town in 1203. Features of interest, including three pubs and a cafe, are all near the junction of the two main streets overlooked by the church. Most interesting building is a former school, endowed by cloth merchant John Brabin in 1683. It sports mullioned windows and forms a tidy group with the adjacent almshouses. St. Bartholomew's church dates from the 16th century, but was restored in Victorian times: great semi-circular steps from the main street are a novel feature. A former cornmill, now a private dwelling, has a restored waterwheel visible from the road bridge on Chipping Brook. Chipping is perhaps best known for its celebrated chairmakers, dating from the 1840s. 1998 saw the first of an annual steam fair at the end of May, while much longer established is the Chipping Show, held in August.

The old watermill, Chipping

STAGE 2

CHIPPING TO CLITHEROE

Distance: 14 miles/22½km

Map:
1:50,000
Landranger 103 - Blackburn & Burnley
1:25,000
Outdoor Leisure 41 - Forest of Bowland & Ribblesdale
Explorer 19 - West Pennine Moors (to be re-numbered)

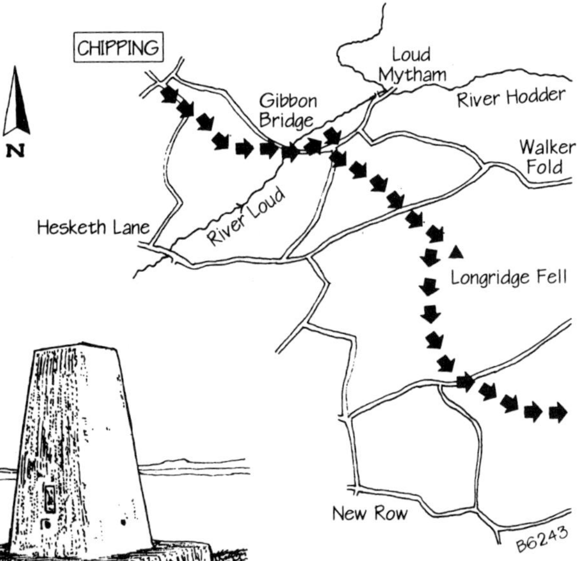

Ordnance Survey column, Longridge Fell, looking to Ingleborough and Penyghent

A truly lovely section through some unsung countryside, relatively little known to walkers outside of Lancashire. The whaleback of Longridge Fell is the principle landmark, and its crossing offers memorable views over a beautiful landscape as we cross from the Vale of Loud, leaving the Bowland scene for the banks of the Ribble and the Hodder. Hurst Green offers a welcoming halfway point, and the splendour of Stonyhurst offers a diversion from some delectable riverbank walking.

•*Transport links: Chipping and Clitheroe are linked by a direct bus service via Longridge. Clitheroe has direct links to Preston, Blackburn, Padiham, Burnley, Nelson, Colne and Skipton, and has trains to Blackburn (for Preston, Burnley, Nelson and Colne) and Manchester. Chipping also has a bus service to Longridge (for Preston).*

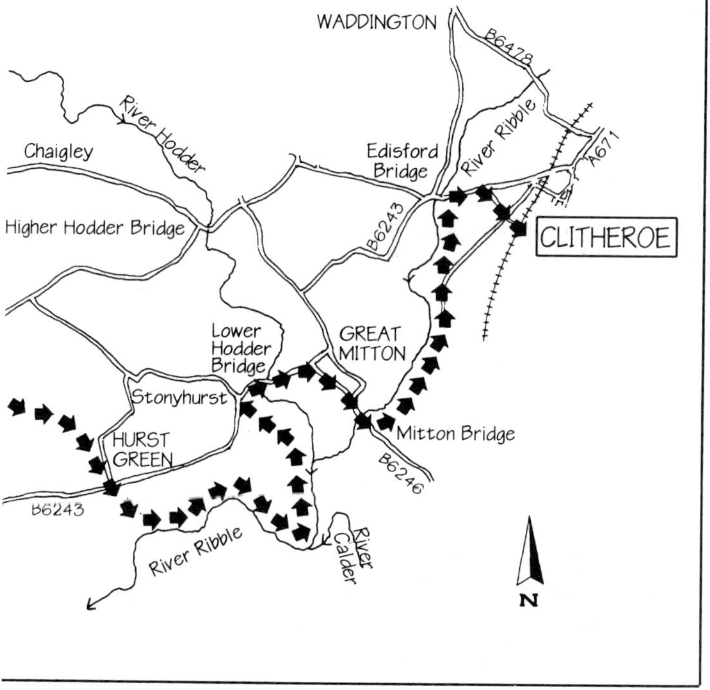

➡ **Depart Chipping along Windy Street, past the *Sun Inn*, and narrowing as it squeezes past the former Brabin's School. Also passing the Roman Catholic church of St. Mary, the road leaves the village at Town End. After the last houses the road bends sharp right. Here go straight ahead over a grassy, stone arched bridge on Chipping Brook, and head away with a fence on the left.** Aptly named Longridge Fell waits ahead.

From the stile at the end maintain this line across the reedy field to a fence corner beneath a few trees. Again, keep this line across an extensive moss, a large enclosure that proves to be surprisingly dry. Pass to the left of a pond in the centre, and advance towards the house at Moss Side in the trees ahead. Look back to see the Bowland fells now ranged from Parlick to Totridge. **From a stile a grassy path runs on to the house, passing left of it and out on the short drive.**

At the T-junction with the access road of Moss Lane cross straight over to the stile in front, and bear left to a fence-stile opposite. Do likewise to reach a stile in the far corner, admitting onto a road. Turn right to reach Gibbon Bridge. Here stands the *Gibbon Bridge Hotel* (originally a farm), where in addition to refreshments you can take advantage of a beauty salon. **Across the bridge take a stile on the left to follow the river Loud downstream.** The lovely Loud is the most unassuming of burbling streams. It joins the Hodder a further half-mile downstream, after an aimless meander between the fells of Bowland and Longridge. **At the end of the second field is a footbridge over a small side-stream. Without crossing, turn upstream to trace the tree-lined brook up to a stile to rejoin the road at a T-junction.**

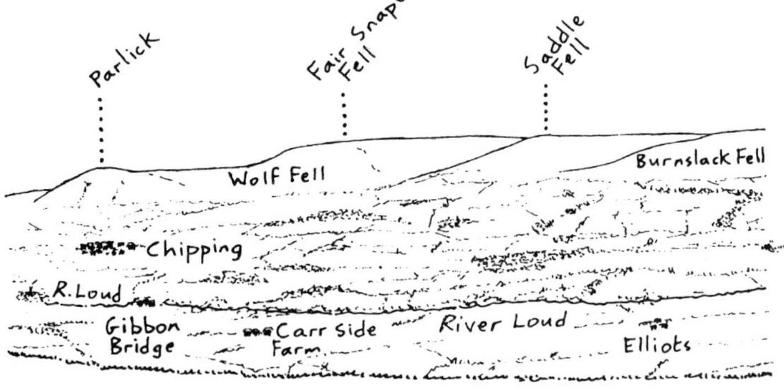

The Bowland moors from Longridge Fell, with a foreground

Go straight across, and up the side road just as far as the first house, Carr Side Farm with its 1833 datestone. After the house take the gate into the farmyard, and pass straight through to two adjacent gates at the end. From the left one, bear left across the field to a protruding fence corner. Go left with the fence as it heads away, but take a stile in a corner before the far corner of the field. Now turn right up the hedgeside, bearing left towards the end to a footbridge in the hedge.

Resume up the fieldside towards the houses at Bradley Court, and again bear left towards the end, passing a fence corner to a stile in front of the houses. Head up the side of the smaller enclosure to a stile and gate onto a short drive. The path is then sent left between the houses, emerging via their access road onto the road. To the left stands Bradley Hall, with a datestone of 1851. On the roadside is an old boundary stone, long since weathered illegible.

Cross straight over to a gate and head away past sheep pens. A stile at the end admits onto the reedy lower slopes of Longridge Fell. Rise with the trees and fence on the left, leaving the rougher ground for a large pasture, and bear gently left up to a gate in the sturdy wall above. From here the true open slopes of the fell are gained, and a short-lived sunken path slants left to meet another old way. Turn right up here for a steady rise to the felltop, the path slanting uniformly up, increasingly through heather. Arrival at the top is quite emphatic, and a path runs straight on to join the ridge wall. Though not essential to the view, normal practice is to detour the two minutes up to the Ordnance Survey column to the left on Spire Hill.

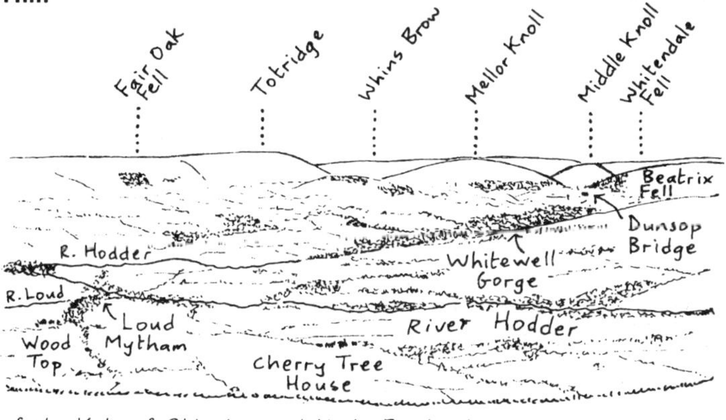

of the Vale of Chipping and Little Bowland

At 1148ft/350m this marks the summit of the country's most southerly named fell. The column sits atop a concrete plinth, and is a place of pilgrimage for West Lancashire walkers. For such a modest height Longridge offers a remarkable panorama. Its complete detachment from other high ground is the key, allied to the fact that the Bowland massif is so near. Across the Vale of Loud, Chipping boasts an idyllic setting, while the wooded meanderings of the Hodder can be traced through green fields liberally scattered with farms. It is the hills that take centre stage, however, for this is surely the ultimate vantage point for Bowland. From Beacon Fell round to Waddington Fell, the glorious heights of Parlick, Fair Snape and Totridge front the great upland dome.

The Way, meanwhile, takes the stile/bridle-gate in the wall ahead, and from the stile just behind, the ways fork. While the broader path bears left, instead take the thinner one slanting gently right through the heather, soon entering a not too claustrophobic tract of conifers. Quickly emerging onto open heather slopes, cross a track and fence-stile as the path slants down to a ladder-stile in a wall corner below. Extensive tracts of heather are still on show over to the right, while Pendle Hill rises over to the left.

The path resumes straight down the moorside to reach the head of a green lane. From the stile descend this very short-lived way to merge into a farm road from Moor Game Hall, and head down this direct course past several houses to emerge onto a road. Sadly now proving elusive is the highly individual sign illustrated herewith, which stood at the foot of this drive.

Under Longridge Fell

Turn left for a good 250 yards, with Pendle Hill returning straight ahead. From a stile on the right slant down the field centre to a stile by an old pond just short of the bottom corner. Maintain the slant over the brow of the next field, passing a recumbent boundary stone on the top, with the letter *B* inscribed. Drop down to a ladder-stile in the bottom corner between two contrasting pockets of woodland.

Ahead now are the copper domed cupolas of Stonyhurst College in front of the Nick of Pendle, while closer to hand is Crowshaw Lodge Reservoir. **Head left down the next field to meet a track at the bottom end.**

Pass right through a stile and the bridleway runs enclosed past a new plantation and into a field. Continuing, it runs along the fieldside with the original overgrown way alongside. Advancing outside the edge of Deer House Wood, a forest track comes in to lead to the farm at Greengore. The architecture of Greengore's central building looks most intriguing, some novel buttresses suggesting an almost fortified style: it dates back several centuries and at one time was a hunting lodge. Currently it functions as a camping barn.

Continue away on the farm road, briefly, but when it swings sharp right keep straight on the far more inviting enclosed green pathway. This runs a grand course, ultimately entering the trees on the left to drop down to stone arched Sandy Bridge. Just yards upstream are waterslides and falls worth viewing. **With chirpy Dean Brook for company, a broader pathway resumes downstream, a wonderful walk with the finest combination of beech woodland and lively waterplay. As the track runs on above waterfalls on the beck, a path branches right to remain with it, quickly arriving at a house.**

Follow the drive rising away and again fork right on a path remaining in the trees. This quickly runs to another drive by some garages. This time follow the drive up onto the road in Hurst Green, opposite the *Bayley Arms*. Just along to the left past the village hall is the Shireburn Almshouse of 1706, an impressive building with various inscriptions and arms, and splendid semi-circular steps. **Turn right for the village centre.**

Hurst Green is a pleasant village indelibly linked with nearby Stonyhurst College. Near the wide junction in the village centre are the Post office/shop and three pubs. The *Eagle & Child* has *'Nuttalls'* windows recalling a defunct Lancashire brewery, while the *Shireburn Hotel* recalls the family that owned Stonyhurst: morning coffee and afternoon tea are on offer. There is a war memorial on the green, while the cross over the road is a less common Boer War memorial. The modest little church of St. John the Evangelist, further west along the road, dates from 1838.

• *STONYHURST COLLEGE*

Stonyhurst College is situated just half a mile from the northern edge of Hurst Green. It is one of the country's leading Roman Catholic boys' schools, with a long history in a beautiful setting. The original Stonyhurst of the Lords Shireburn began in the late 14th century: their Elizabethan manor house was started by Sir Richard Shireburn, and the gatehouse dates from 1592. Oliver Cromwell is reputed to have stayed the night before the Battle of Preston in 1648. The family line was lost in 1717, and after some neglect it was handed to the Society of Jesus in 1794. In the mid-19th century much extension work took place, and St. Peter's church was built in 1835.

Facing the West front are two serene ponds beloved of waterfowl, flanking the main drive which leads out along a broad avenue. The school is open to visitors (admission fee) on afternoons in the main Summer holidays, though the only Monday is at the Bank Holiday. In addition to the architectural features and all-round history, the house has countless priceless treasures. The gardens open earlier in July. There is also a teashop and gift shop.

West Front, Stonyhurst College

At Hurst Green we leave the Forest of Bowland AONB for the next few miles, though the landscape quality suffers nothing from its lack of designation. **From the war memorial, cross the main road and turn into the car park of the *Shireburn Hotel*. Descend to a wall-stile by a gate, and head down the field with a hedge on the right.** There are good views over the valley, with Pendle Hill to the left and the 'Whalley Arches' viaduct discernible beneath Whalley Nab. **When the fence turns off right, cross the fledgling stream and resume on a well defined tongue between miniature streams. From a stile at the bottom a path passes through a few trees, then bear left outside the wood to find a stile at the end.** Here the Ribble Way is joined, and remains our course too for the ensuing six miles to Edisford Bridge on the edge of Clitheroe.

The path descends left through woodland to a bridge on a sidestream. Beyond this the riverbank is gained, to follow the Ribble upstream. At once the graceful arches of an aqueduct are passed. Ahead, the great bulk of Pendle Hill is dominant, and will remain in view for many of the ensuing miles. **The way is now foolproof for some time, as we simply trace the riverbank upstream. Just before joining a drive look back to the left: the cross on the brow is a 19th century shaft in an older base. The drive leads to the farm at Jumbles.**

Without entering, turn right on the track to quickly regain the riverbank, and continue upstream. The modest scars that break the river's flow are known as Jumbles Rocks: enjoy also an extensive view downstream. **A kissing-gate sees us into a lush riverbank pasture, and a great loop of the river ensues. This is a fine moment as the splendid Hacking Hall appears directly ahead.** With its imposing five gables this hoary old place dates from 1607. The fact that it actually stands on the opposite bank is not immediately apparent.

The more modest, isolated building just ahead is a former boatman's house. This was in regular use when the Hacking Ferry plied the river. A small passenger boat operated well into the 1950s, and one of the old ferryboats is on display in the Castle Museum, Clitheroe. **Just beyond the old house make for the riverbank, where an anglers' refuge overlooks the confluence of Burnley's river Calder with the Ribble.** At some future date a long envisaged footbridge might be built to 'replace' the ferry. If this materialises, it will be joined by an adjacent bridge on the Calder, thus allowing what is at present a cul-de-sac path to be used for a more direct route towards Mitton Bridge.

Resuming upstream, further riverside rambling leads to meet a track which comes in to take us along to Winckley Hall Farm. Prior to the farm is a vantage point where we part company with the Ribble, as it turns away with the Big End of Pendle directly behind. Approaching the farm, the sudden realisation that we still have a river for company will catch out those not doing their homework, for now it is the lovely Hodder that glides quietly alongside.

Turn into the farmyard, past the big house. Little remains of its Elizabethan origins, though some old windows hide round the back. The lovely L-shaped pond is the remains of a moat. **Rise up the drive. Outside the grounds of the red-brick Winckley Hall, take an iron kissing-gate on the right and cross straight over the field to another. Here a second field is crossed to the wood on the right, then the field edge followed.** Part way along, on the brow, the copper domed cupolas of Stonyhurst are seen, rising across the fields. **From the stile at the end two shorter field-sides lead to a road junction.** This untidy diversion away from the river is unavoidable in the absence of rights of way.

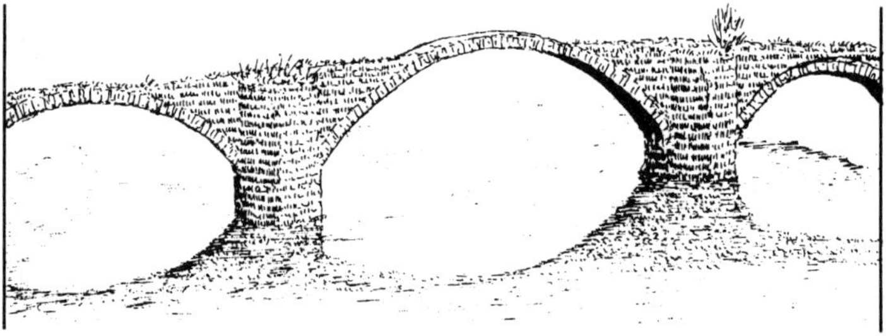

Cromwell's Bridge on the river Hodder

Turn right along the road on a much appreciated footway down to Lower Hodder Bridge. With one eye on the traffic look downstream to the three arches of the remarkable Cromwell's Bridge, so named as the great historical figure passed this way prior to the Battle of Preston in 1648. It was built by a member of the Shireburn family in the 16th century. Upstream, meanwhile, is a delightful prospect of the Hodder. **Across the bridge remain on the road which climbs to a junction, and with the church tower of Great Mitton beckoning, turn right to shortly enter this tiny village.**

• *GREAT MITTON*

Great Mitton offers refuge to all, at the *Three Fishes* pub or the tearoom in front of the church. The church of All Hallows with its superb old tower dates from the 14th century. Inside is a splendid pre-Reformation screen which came from Sawley Abbey, while the Shireburn family chapel dates from 1594 and boasts an amazing assembly of recumbent effigies. Adjacent to the church is the Old Hall with its mullioned windows, and this too dates back in part to the 14th century. Great Mitton is truly a Yorkshire outpost: here the traditional, all-embracing West Riding burrows deep into the heart of Lancashire. Both the Ribble and Hodder, which meet just downstream, form the real county boundary.

All Hallows church, Great Mitton: Pendle Hill behind

Keep straight on past the hall and down the road to cross Mitton Bridge. Downstream, the Ribble glides over low rocky shelves, while upstream it leads the eye to Pendle Hill. Note also, while crossing, the fine setting of Great Mitton's old hall and church on their knoll is well appreciated now. At the bridge end is the *Aspinall Arms*, its traditional inn sign, recalling a once important local family, echoed more individually on the front of the building itself. Yet more refreshment is available just 100 yards further at Mitton Hall. Currently its public bar *Owd Ned's Tavern* serves food all day.

Immediately past the *Aspinall Arms* a kissing-gate points the way upstream. The thin path follows the field edge to the far end, deflected by a wooded bank above the river. A further field-side and kissing-gate lead on to a footbridge over a beck, to then enter a large riverside pasture. Bear left across to the small waterworks building from where a grassy track runs upstream to a shapely aqueduct. Continue upstream on a broad track which leads to Shuttleworth Farm. Pass left of the buildings to follow the drive out past several houses - including the curiously named Fishes and Peggy Hill - and continue upstream beneath the well screened local refuse site. The river here disappears in a great bow, backed by the tree-cloaked eastern end of Longridge Fell. Our road heads straight on, absorbing the tip road.

Just past the lone Mill House here, a popular path slips into the trees on the left, following the beck upstream to escape the tip waggons. It rejoins the road at a stone arched bridge. Just beyond, turn left along the drive towards Siddows Farm. At the early fork, go right a few yards then take a kissing-gate on the left, crossing a small field (Clitheroe's castle keep is clearly seen on its knoll from this brow) to one at the far corner. From here a path slants down to the river, which is followed upstream to Edisford Bridge, a mile from Clitheroe town centre on the B6243 Hurst Green road.

On our right a caravan site is well screened, and the popular riverside picnic area is soon reached, passing a miniature railway (Ribble Valley Live Steamers) en route. Toilets too, and a cafe: it's all here! Edisford (older name Eadsford) Bridge was the scene of a skirmish in 1138 between Scots and Normans. Prior to the ancient bridge, a ford existed here on the Clitheroe-Lancaster medieval way. Just across the river stands the *Edisford Bridge Inn*. **For both the town centre and the through route, simply join the road and turn right.**

Mitton Bridge and the River Ribble
On the lower slopes of Pendle Hill

Lothersdale, hidden in a fold of the hills

The moors above the Worth Valley, Haworth

• *CLITHEROE*

The bustling market town of Clitheroe sits at the heart of a vast rural area - its market charter goes back to 1283. Focal point is the castle remains, which date from the late 12th century. The Norman keep watches over both the town and the valley from the natural motte of its limestone knoll, and is perhaps the smallest in the country. Open to visitors, the climb to the top is rewarded with a superb Ribble Valley prospect featuring the brooding mass of Pendle Hill. This one situation perfectly encapsulates Clitheroe's important setting.

Within the grounds of the castle a popular museum exhibits much of local interest, while Clitheroe Castle Fayre takes place annually, with mock battles amongst its attractions. The church of St. Mary Magdalene boasts a 15th century tower, while on the edge of town are the acclaimed Geology Trail at Salthill Quarry, and a Sculpture Trail by the river.

¶ To rejoin the route from the town centre: from the principle shopping thoroughfare of Castle Street, turn left down Moor Lane in front of the Castle entrance. At the *Brown Cow* bear right on Woone Lane, remain on this to Primrose Mill at the far end, here meeting the through route.

'Saving Sheep' by Thompson Dagnall, on the riverbank sculpture trail

STAGE 3

CLITHEROE TO EARBY

Distance: 15 miles/24km

Map:
1:50,000
Landranger 103 -
Blackburn & Burnley
1:25,000
Outdoor Leisure 21 -
South Pennines
Outdoor Leisure 41 -
Forest of Bowland & Ribblesdale

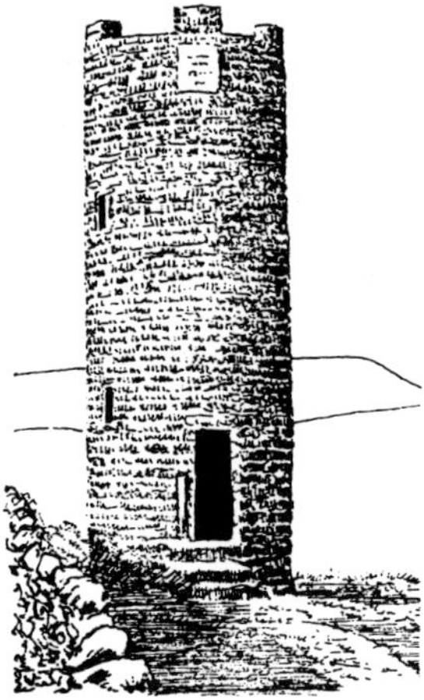

Stansfield Tower, Blacko Hill

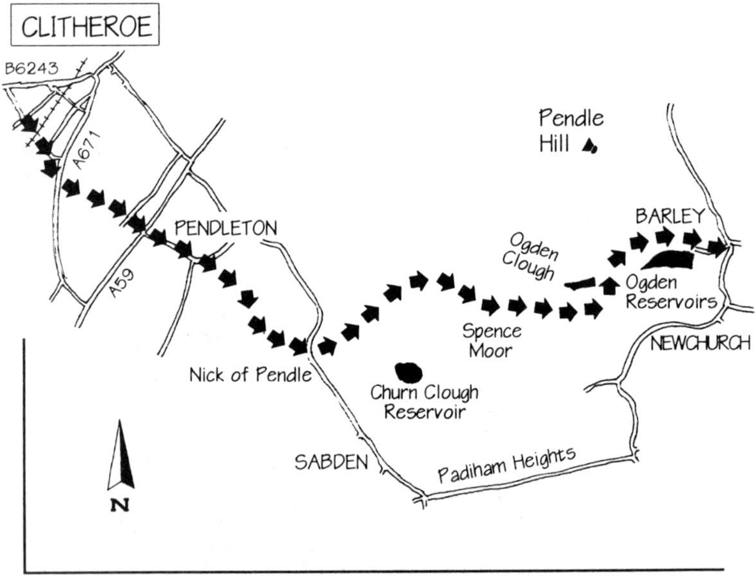

From the Ribble Valley to the Witch Country, mighty Pendle Hill beats at the heart of this stage, and is in sight and thoughts for most of the day. The crossing of its southern shoulder incorporates the high point of the TPW, and there is an alternative route to take in the very summit of the hill for the more ambitious.

• *Transport links: Clitheroe has direct bus links to Preston, Blackburn, Padiham, Burnley, Nelson, Colne and Skipton, and has trains to Blackburn (for Preston, Burnley, Nelson and Colne) and Manchester. Earby is served by Colne-Skipton buses (both towns have railway stations).*

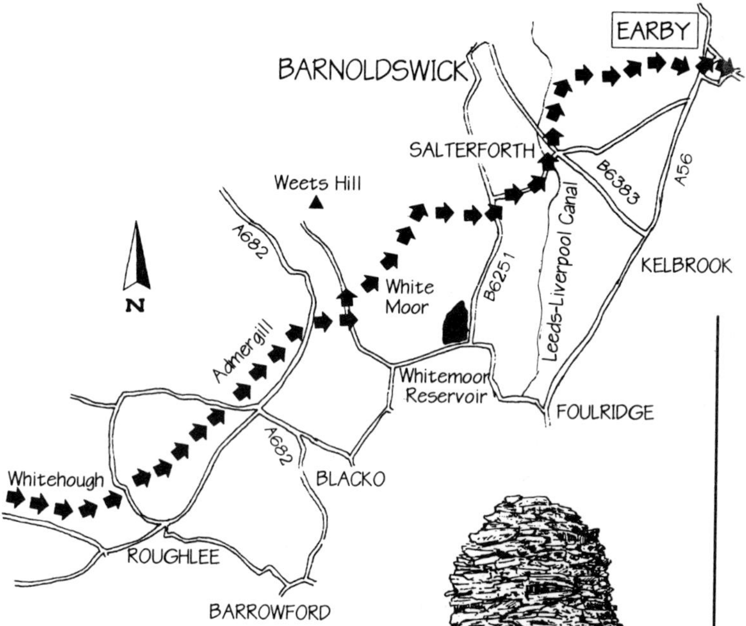

The Scout Cairn, Pendle Hill

➡ **From Edisford Bridge the through route advances towards the town centre, but turns right along suburban Lancaster Drive opposite the imposing church of St. Paul's at Low Moor. Continue on as Garnett Road to a crossroads at the end. Cross and resume along Mytton View to meet Kemple View, where a tall footbridge crosses the railway.** This is the line from Blackburn to Clitheroe, which continues to Hellifield where it meets the celebrated Leeds-Settle-Carlisle line. The bridge also offers a view to the castle keep.

Across the bridge, a snicket heads away to join a rough road alongside Primrose Mill, and thence onto Woone Lane. Turn right, passing a sizeable millpond on the left. As the road swings sharp left, now as Primrose Road, turn right along a rough road after the mill to enter the yard at Lower Standen. After the house turn left along the access road out onto the A671. Go right just 50 yards after Lower Standen, and cross to a stile and gate opposite. Head away with the hedge, on through successive kissing-gates to enter an extensive tract of Standen Hall's parkland. Maintain the same line across the centre to join an enclosed cart track. Go right on this which leads pleasantly out to a road junction.

Cross straight over along the short-lived road onto the A56 Clitheroe bypass. On the skyline directly ahead is our next objective, the Nick of Pendle. **Cross with care and escape along the side road to Pendleton. This quickly enters the village to reveal a delightful scene.** A stream runs through the centre, with numerous attractive cottages and a pub, the *Swan with Two Necks*, set back. A 1693 datestone sits above a cottage window as the village is entered. Here we also re-enter the Forest of Bowland AONB, now within the entirely detached section based on Pendle Hill. **Keep on to the head of the village, to just short of a small green by the little church.** A dwelling on the left is the former National School of 1837, rebuilt in 1870.

Just before the church bear right on a cart track, leading to a pair of gates by an old building that was clearly once more than a basic barn. From the stile by the right-hand gate head up the long field, close to the tree-lined stream on the right. Passing through some curious hollows a footbridge on the beck is reached. Across it, slant up to the hedge above, and follow it left until reaching a stile in it. Just to our left is the colourful Swardean Clough, while the *Wellsprings Inn* is now very clear high on Pendle's flank, with a dry ski slope alongside. **Cross the short field top to a stile then turn uphill again, an old hawthorn hedge leading along to the farm at Wymondhouses.**

From a wall-stile pass to the left of the house and head up the rough pasture behind. Look back to see the old house with its mullioned windows: dating from the 17th century, it is the survivor of what was once a larger settlement. **An old way slants up to a stile in a gateway in the wall above.** Pause here to look back over the Ribble Valley backed by the diminishing prospect and memories of Parlick. **The stile accesses an old sunken way, which shadows the wall uphill across the grassy moor. At the top it rises to a wall junction, and from the stile/gate it continues up a final pasture to swing left to emerge at a gate onto the crest of the Sabden road at the Nick of Pendle.**

Go right a few yards and cross to the broad track directly opposite. This heads off firmly and decisively along the crest of the broad moorland ridge. With no navigational problems and superb walking, just stride out and enjoy the wide views. Prominent over to the right are our next objective the Deerstones. **This moorland track links ancient Bronze Age sites, one being the scrappy pile of stones which we climb to on Apronfull Hill.** The prospect to the south looks over Churn Clough Reservoir and the nearby village of Sabden down in its near-hidden valley, to the Pennine moors above the string of East Lancashire mill towns centred upon Burnley.

Deerstones, near Spence Moor

On Apronfull Hill there is an option to remain on the main path bound for Pendle Hill's summit, and thence rejoin the main route in Barley: see panel overleaf. The main route continues on page 40.

• ***PENDLE HILL***

On the Pendle Hill alternative, note that only the first and last miles are on public rights of way: please respect the linking concessionary paths.

While the main route of the Way branches off for Deerstones, the main path underfoot forges on up the slopes. A pile of stones on a brow signals the revelation of Pendle's great expanse, vast moorland slopes culminating in the broad summit - no inclination of Pendle's familiar Big End outline here! At a major brow in the saddle linking with Spence Moor to the right, Ogden Clough takes shape ahead, a fine foreground to the great dome of the summit area behind. As the track turns upstream with it, there are fine views back down the steep sided clough.

Approaching a crumbling wall, transfer to a path that has developed on the right, to run along the inside of the clough. A grand path shadows the stream tumbling over stony ledges. In time the clough eases and path and brook come together. Just yards beyond a free-standing boundary stone inscribed *WA*, with a wall in view ahead, the path crosses the brook to a cairn and climbs away through eroded peat groughs. Looking back, there is nothing but moorland. The gradient quickly eases but the peat relents less readily. Only as the Ordnance Survey column on Pendle's summit appears does the terrain improve, finishing over bare stony turf.

Arrival on a summit is always a good moment, and here we have the added bonus of the hitherto unseen view eastwards. There can be no day of the year when no-one ventures up, and the likelihood is that there will be many folk here, for almost everyone uses the Barley 'tourist' path, usually both up and down. First reward is a perch on the rim of the mighty drop, enjoying a bird's-eye view over Barley as it nestles in its fold of the hills. Pendle's isolation ensures extensive views in all directions, with the South and West Pennine Moors beyond the East Lancashire conurbations, a long Dales line-up to the north, and a Bowland skyline to the west.

Leave by following the path north to a gate and ladder-stile in the prominent wall. Here the main highway, strengthened to counter the thousands of feet, reveals itself and slants down to a gate at the foot of the fell. Slant across behind Pendle House to a stile from where the thin path descends the field to a gate. Bear right down the next field to a stile part-way down, and a little path runs down to the white-fronted Brown House. Go straight ahead to an old iron kissing-gate, and resume down the field-side on a lovely path by a tiny stream. This becomes enclosed at the bottom. Emerging onto a lane go left a short way, then at a bend take a wooden footbridge on the right. Turn down the field, which proves to be the final one as Barley's rooftops appear just ahead. At the far corner a small footbridge is crossed before the path becomes enclosed for the final yards onto Barley's main street.

While Pendle may indeed be indelibly linked with the Ribble, it claims a far more sinister connection. It all happened in a small area in the eastern shadow of the hill. The events of 1612 have been glamorised into the classic witch story of the north, and the subject of several novels. It began with a young girl suspected of foul play, quickly spread to her family, involved the local magistrate Squire Nowell of Read Hall, and resulted in an extended group being taken to Lancaster for trial and subsequent hanging. The very names of the supposed ringleaders strike a chill on a mist-wreathed day on Pendle. The surprise catch among the likes of Old Demdike and Old Chattox was Alice Nutter, a 'respectable' lady from Roughlee Hall.

Pendle Forest was established as an 11th century hunting forest covering the country south from the hill towards Colne. The hill has for centuries also been a beacon site, when a chain of fires would warn of approaching danger. Its busiest day might well be Good Friday, when it seems the whole of East Lancashire pulls on its boots to take Bank Holiday exercise. Needless to say, Hallowe'en is also a busy time for revellers. The hill is parcelled into various moors, though anyone up there is simply 'on Pendle'.

A cairn on Pendle Hill

After a few near-level minutes from Apronfull Hill, a green track branches off right for Deerstones, contouring round to a stile/gate in the sturdy ascending wall. Across it, a concession path offers an alternative route by simply remaining with the wall. Preferably, head directly away on the slender but clear footpath running a level, embanked course to arrive above the edge of Deerstones. The path now scales the gentle edge to quickly reach the highest point of the edge. The few modest outcrops at the Deerstones overlook a deep, boulder-filled amphitheatre, and make an impressive foreground to an extensive view.

The way ahead involves a slight descent, aiming for a prominent ladder-stile on the skyline eastwards. An unofficial alternative is to simply cross directly to join the wallside concession path, just yards away. From the stile a path heads directly away across Spence Moor, initially rather moist. It soon picks up, and enjoys a fine march. On the brow the summit of the moor, and indeed the summit of the entire Trans-Pennine Way, is reached at a fairly unexceptional 1509ft/460m. The great prow of Pendle looms across to our left, leaving us unaware of the deep, intervening Ogden Clough. The extensive panorama ahead features Burn Moor, Barden Moor, Skipton Moor, Earl Crag, Boulsworth Hill and a vast sweep round the South Pennines to the West Pennine Moors; additionally, there are final glimpses back to Longridge Fell and Bowland.

The path begins its descent by angling down to the wall, where a ladder-stile awaits. From it descend a less appealing section, keeping left of a reedy line alongside a long crumbled wall. There is no complete escape from the mire here until reaching, with relief, a stile by a gate at the bottom. Head away to the left on a clear path contouring across the sloping moor. The Black Moss reservoirs appear over to the left beneath Burn Moor, while further to the left Pendle improves in shape.

The path leads to a stile in an intervening fence and old wall on Driver Height, and continues in similar fashion to an identical arrangement a little further. This time turn left down its near side, or to avoid some initially marshy moments, perhaps a little before it. Either way, moisture is sure to be encountered as Ogden Clough is fully revealed below, featuring the higher, more dramatically sited of its two reservoirs. Further left, the upper reaches of Ogden Clough carve a deep defile between bracken-clad flanks.

At the bottom a stile gives access to the grassy embankment of Upper Ogden Reservoir. Completed in 1906, its 7 acres are a mere third of the extent of its lower neighbour, yet its location in this deep-cut valley ensures it boasts the same capacity. **Across it, join a firm access track and turn right. An uncomplicated walk leads out into Barley village, passing en route along the length of Lower Ogden Reservoir, opened eight years after its higher neighbour.** Barley is entered at Barley Green, where a great mill was destroyed by floods in 1880, and replaced with great irony by Nelson's waterworks.

On emerging, go left a few yards along the village street. Barley is an unassuming village that bears the brunt of Pendle-seekers, with a stream for kids to dabble in, and ice creams on offer. There is a pub, the *Pendle Inn*, and a restaurant, as well as a Post office/shop. An information centre at the car park is open in season and at winter weekends, also serving refreshments. There are toilets alongside. The car park occupies the site of an old mill dam, for being so near the larger settlements the village was also caught up in the Industrial Revolution: cotton mills and earlier small-scale handloom weaving meant this was a busy little spot.

Barley, looking to Pendle Hill

From the pub cross the road to a small footbridge from where a path runs into an open area leading to the car park and information centre. At the far end of the car park a path enters trees to immediately join a broad track: go left on this old road to quickly enter the hamlet of Narrowgates. This, incidentally, is the old road to Barley, long since replaced by the modern, parallel one across the stream; it is also the route of the Pendle Way. First feature is a preserved stone square chimney at the remains of the cotton mill, closed in the 1960s. The old way then passes through two attractive rows of former weavers' cottages, restored in the 1970s. **Beyond Narrowgates this old road, now as a bridleway, runs downstream in grand surrounds.**

At the houses at Whitehough, turn sharp left up the access road. On the right is Whitehough Farm, with some lovely mullioned windows and a 1593 datestone. A youth hostel existed at Whitehough from 1943 to 1965. **After the houses the road swings up to the right. Before the top, watch for a stile on the right after a small red-brick building. The path runs on through lovely beechwood beneath the grounds of Whitehough Camp School.** This popular outdoor centre has been run for several decades by Lancashire Education Authority.

Emerging into a contrastingly open field, rise left to the buildings at Intake Farm. There are now extensive views over the hidden valley of Pendle Water to a long Pennine skyline, reaching from Kelbrook Moor southwards past Boulsworth Hill. Looking back, Ogden Clough is well seen between its enclosing arms of the Pendle massif. **From the corner stile the Way is deflected up around the external boundary of the house's grounds. Dropping back onto its drive, go left out onto the road.**

Turn uphill to a sharp bend, then right on another access road, to Hollin Top. Passing under Brown Hill, this offers further grand views over Colne to the South Pennine watershed. En route, the Pendle Way leaves us. **Approaching the house, bear left of its confines to a stile in the wall just above. Passing behind the first house to a gate, ignore the green track rising away, and continue straight on along a thinner path (behind the house) to a stile in the wall. Cross the field top above Bank End Wood, and at the end advance on to a barn.**

Passing round into the barn's yard, leave through a gateway on the right, just to the right of a corner stile which is ignored. Head away with a wall on the right, initially on a stone flagged path. As the wall turns off keep straight on this pleasant open crest. At the end drop towards the top corner of the wood, and an old iron gate/gap-stile await in front. Pause here to appraise a glorious prospect, with Stansfield Tower on Blacko Hill looking very impressive straight ahead, then round into the Admergill valley, and left again to Burn Moor's heathery crest. Pendle Hill's own crest can just be glimpsed over the left shoulder.

From the stile continue straight down through new plantings to a stile below, with the house at Bank End just over to the right. Resume straight down another area of scattered young conifers, using stiles to cross an 'internal' fence. Aim slightly left of the landmark of Stansfield Tower to drop to a stile at the bottom. Cross a side-stream, and with the main beck over to the right, rise up the field to find a stile beneath a telegraph pole. With another stile just behind it, slant down the field to join the road via stone steps at a red-brick bridge. Here we take our final leave of the Forest of Bowland AONB, and at the same time rejoin the Pendle Way. **Cross the road, not the bridge, and descend steps to a slab bridge at a confluence. Over the side-stream, follow Admergill Water upstream on a slim green path.**

Through several pastures we approach the hamlet at Lower Admergill. Before the first house (Admergill Barn), the path has been diverted to cross the prominent footbridge on the right, and resumes up-stream to a gate into the grounds of the house. Go right out on the drive, and right over a cattle-grid and bridge. At the first bend, take the drive along to the left to Admergill Hall Farm. On crossing the beck en route, note the old slab bridge: a deep groove in the centre indicates regular usage in packhorse days. The hall itself is a splendid old house, with leaning mullioned windows, some arch-headed.

Keep straight on the drive until it turns up to the left by a seat, with Burn Moor rising high above. Keep straight on upstream, through pleasant mixed pasture and past wildlife ponds to arrive at two stiles. That on the left gives access to Countryside Stewardship land, an appealing bracken-clad patch where visitors are welcome to amble about. This is home to upland ground nesting birds such as snipe and curlew, and a breeding ground for brown hares.

Take the right-hand stile, cross a slab bridge and climb steeply up the bank, bound for the gate on the skyline. Super views over the upper reaches of this side valley are enjoyed. **Near the top the faint path slants across to the gate, using a stile to emerge onto the A682. Just along to the left, the *Moorcock Inn* offers a possible detour. From the stile opposite, however, a path slants up to a wall corner with a farm behind.**

Bear left with the wall to a gate in front of Admergill Pasture Farm. Don't advance to the house itself, but go straight up the yard to a pair of stiles at the top. From the left-hand one a path rises by a wall and old sunken way, and on from another stile up to the top end of the sunken way. Here we leave the Pendle Way, only encountering it again very briefly on the streets of Earby. **Don't cross the stile here but go a few yards to the right, where another stile and gate send a short-lived, enclosed green way out onto Gisburn Old Road. Go left on this quiet, gently rising back road.**

Gisburn Old Road was a major packhorse route prior to the construction of the turnpike below - the present A682 road. Northwards from here it climbs onto Weets Hill and runs a short barely discernible section before resuming as Coal Pit Lane for the last stage to Gisburn. We currently have some fine views back over Burn Moor to Pendle Hill. **Our Way follows the old road only briefly however, and just beyond the isolated Peel's House take a kissing-gate on the right. Head away with the wall, sections of boarding assisting through moister moments as this reedy way lead along to the terminus of the walled green lane of Lister Well Road.**

Lister Well Road provides a gem of a stroll alongside the rampant heather carpet of White Moor. The way remains a classic as heather moorland rapidly envelops our way, even down to this green road's verges. This way rolls on for some time, gradually declining until commencing a more pronounced descent. Here, from a stile by a gate on the right, head off on a more inviting track down the heather moor. Ahead is the next stage's objective of Pinhaw on Elslack Moor, the village of Kelbrook beneath its own pocket moor, and our more immediate goals of Salterforth and Earby.

As the track swings right to a pond, continue down to the gate below to leave the moor. Descend the pasture to a gate/stile in the corner below, and an arrow-like green way descends to the farm at Copy Nook. Its drive continues downhill, still in grand fashion, to emerge onto the B6251 Barnoldswick-Foulridge road. Rather handily the *Fanny Grey* pub stands alongside, and its tempting garden offers lovely views across the valley.

Go left a few yards along the road and then turn down the side road for Salterforth. This leads quickly down to the Leeds-Liverpool Canal and adjacent pub on the edge of Salterforth. En route we pass a garden centre with a cafe, and then Higher Greenhill Farm with a large 1768 datestone. Yet more refreshment is on offer at the *Anchor Inn,* a celebrated canalside pub. Dating back several centuries it was astride an old salt way, and thus a regular halt in packhorse times. Transported all over the north from mines in Cheshire, salt was important for preserving meat, and indeed it gave the village its name from the simple translation of 'salters' ford'. The original pub, the *Travellers Rest,* was in fact at a lower level, but construction of the canal made a higher level building necessary. The pub is also renowned for its cellar, which features stalagtite formations as a result of its damp situation beneath the canal. The rest of the village is just across the main road beyond.

The Anchor Inn, Salterforth

The Leeds-Liverpool Canal runs a 127¼ mile course between its two great city termini, and is the northernmost of three trans-Pennine waterways. Unlike its counterparts further south, which tunnelled deep below the hills, this one took advantage of the low-level Aire Gap to breach the Pennines by way of a chain of locks. Begun in 1770 and fully opened in 1816 for what proved to be a short-lived industrial use, it was overtaken during the course of the 19th century by the arrival of the railways. Today it is a vibrant leisure amenity, catering for walkers, bargees, anglers, naturalists, and in places, cyclists.

The Way takes to the canal towpath opposite the pub (left), and heads away past the colourful moorings. The canal passes under the B6383 Barnoldswick-Kelbrook road at Park Bridge, and is followed as far as the next arched canal bridge, Cockshutt Bridge, alongside

which is Lower Park Marina (refreshments). En route we pass the embankment and a forlorn stone abutment of the Barnoldswick branch line. Opened in 1871, it ran for less than two miles from a junction with the old Skipton-Colne railway at Sough, just south of Earby. The line closed in 1965, a casualty of Dr. Beeching's infamous axe. Modern maps still show the railway bridge in place.

Only a mile or so further along the towpath is the independent little town of Barnoldswick, known locally as 'Barlick'. Though something of a backwater between Skipton and Colne, it is an important site of local employment thanks to two large factories. The centre boasts a wide range of services for its size, with the modern Town Square as focal point. Along with neighbouring Earby, Barnoldswick is a part of Yorkshire gone temporarily missing after the 1974 boundary revisions, though as these are strictly local government changes, it is generally accepted as still being part of real Yorkshire.

The route shuns both the canal and the bridge, and goes through a stile/gate on the right. A grassy path follows the wall directly away to another stile, then slant left across the bottom of a minor grassy ravine. Continue up the slope, past its top end and on to a stile onto the roughly surfaced Salterforth Lane. Head straight off along the drive opposite, to Kayfield. Entering the farmyard, advance to a gate straight in front then on through two small enclosures linked by stiles. Cross the next field to a gate/gap-stile at the far right corner, then bear left to a stile at the end. This marks a junction of numerous paths, and reveals a clear prospect of the rolling Pennine slopes.

Ignoring an adjacent stile, bear gently away from the left-hand hedge, soon reaching the brow of the large field to reveal Earby in all its glory. Drop left to the bottom of the field, some way to the right of the solitary house at Hill Top. From the stile in the fence descend the fieldside to merge into the house's drive, which then continues downhill to pass under the old railway to meet the A56 Colne-Skipton road in Earby. Opened in 1848 the railway was once a vital Yorkshire-Lancashire link, and though it narrowly survived the Beeching cuts, its closure in 1970 left Colne a cul-de-sac and Skipton no longer a junction.

Earby is the smaller cousin of Barnoldswick, and presents a rather odd centre, where public houses are at a premium. It is best known for its Museum of Yorkshire Dales Lead Mining. Delightfully housed in the

400-year old former grammar school, it is dedicated to preserving and displaying artifacts and information on the once-thriving lead mining industry in the nearby Yorkshire Dales. Operated by volunteers, it is normally open April/Easter to October, Wednesday-Sunday 1.00-5.00; Thursday 1.00-8.00.

Go left a few yards and cross to head off along Albion Road, joining the shopping row of Victoria Road. Go left on this to the end, passing the little bus station. The Museum is just two minutes to the left along School Lane, past the big works of Wardle Storey's. **The Way turns right past further shops, and keeps left along Water Street.** At this junction a pub, the *White Lion*, can be found two minutes along to the right. **Water Street becomes Red Lion Street and duly passes the pub of that name. It continues as Moor Brow Road, then Birch Hall Lane, and at a tight corner reaches the youth hostel.** The cosy Glen Cottage has served countless thousands of walkers since it was opened in 1955, many detouring from the nearby Pennine Way. It is known as the Katharine Bruce Glasier Memorial Hostel, recalling its former occupant, an early 20th century politician of note.

At the lead mining museum, Old Grammar School, Earby

•*Transport links: Earby is served by Colne-Skipton buses (both towns have railway stations). Haworth is served by bus from Keighley and Bradford. It is also linked to Keighley by the Worth Valley Railway. Keighley has trains to Bradford, Leeds, Skipton and beyond.*

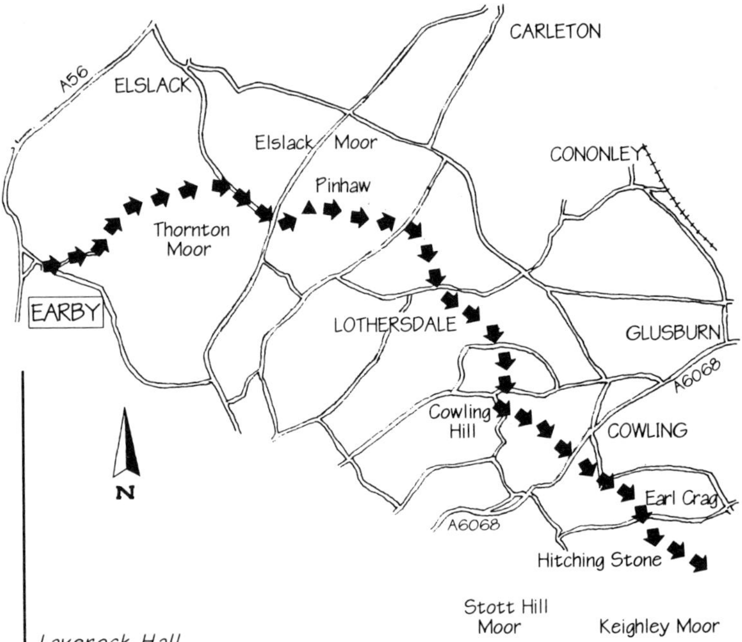

Laverock Hall, near Oldfield

STAGE 4

EARBY TO HAWORTH

Distance: 14 miles/22½km

Map:
1:50,000
Landranger 103 - Blackburn & Burnley
Landranger 104 - Leeds, Bradford & Harrogate
1:25,000
Outdoor Leisure 21 - South Pennines

Today marks the true Pennine watershed crossing: Lancashire into Yorkshire, west to east, but it's not all downhill from now on! Though Lothersdale is a tempting place to linger over an early beer, remember there are a lot of ups and downs before the day is done. The heather moorland of Pinhaw Beacon and the dramatic edge of Earl Crag are major highlights between the gritstone villages culminating in the Brontë shrine of Haworth.

Earl Crag from Eastburn

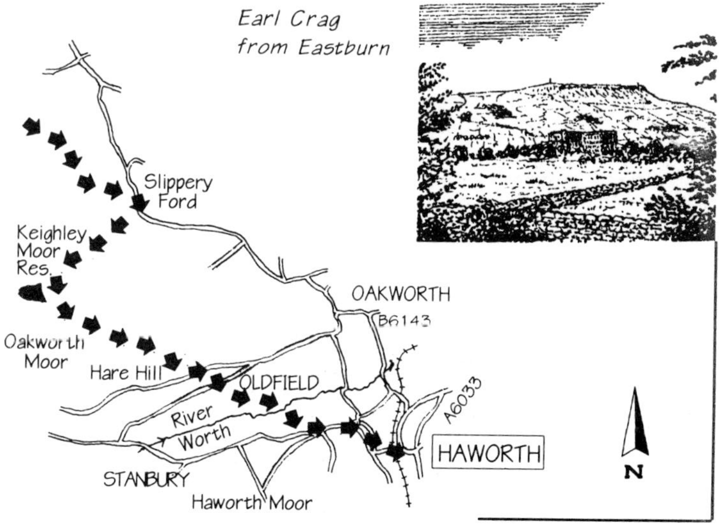

➡ **Resuming the walk at the youth hostel, turn along the rough lane immediately after it. Before the car park, however, take a gap-stile on the left and a little path runs through the trees to a footbridge on Wentcliff Brook. Across, it slant away from the beck, up the fieldside and up past a largely destroyed hedge to a prominent stile in the wall above. Joining the access road of Gaylands Lane, turn right to rise steadily uphill.** Ever improving views look back over Earby to the previous stage, while to the right are the imminent moors of the Pennine watershed.

Simply remain on this to the house at Thornton Highgate. En route we cross the modern boundary from Lancashire into North Yorkshire. **A little above the house the rough road forks. Take the left branch through the gate, and continue rising to a sharp bend with the isolated house at The Mount to the left. At this junction of ways take the gate in front, onto a corner of Thornton Moor. A splendid track heads away, keeping close to the right-hand wall.** Ahead, our goal of Pinhaw rises above heather moorland.

On a minor brow the track veers away from the wall and forks. The right branch, seen striding out across the moor, is the direct and most commonly used route to link the Pennine Way with the youth hostel. It rises pleasantly to arrive at a gate/stile and wall-corner at the far end. Here the Pennine Way is also joined for the next 2½ miles into Lothersdale. The public footpath takes the left branch, a broad, seldom used track that swings sharp right at a fork at the back of Stone Pit Hill, and soon fades on another minor brow. A fainter way then works left to meet the Pennine Way path alongside the moor edge wall. This too leads on to the stile at the wall corner.

From the stile the path runs on to merge into a moorland road amid some lovely tracts of heather, most notably over the wall on Thornton Moor. The road rises gently to a T-junction with the old Skipton-Colne road. This moorland highway was once the major route linking the two towns, more direct and less hazardous than the valley route that ultimately replaced it. **Straight across, a good track heads away with the wall, then swings away from it at a corner for the very short rise between the heathery knolls of Elslack Moor to the waiting Ordnance Survey column on Pinhaw.**

Despite a modest altitude of 1273ft/388m, Pinhaw is the highest point in the northernmost tract of the South Pennines. As a result it boasts an extensive 360° panorama, with the Yorkshire Dales fells to the north being the finest feature - keen eyes might also pick out the limestone cliff of Malham Cove. Without its modern adornments of trig. point and cairn, the summit remains highly distinguishable as the raised site of a beacon. Like Beacon Fell and Pendle Hill on earlier stages of the Way, this would have been one of a long chain that stretched across the country centuries ago, to warn of impending danger and also celebrate major events.

Pinhaw Beacon, looking back to Pendle Hill

Resume eastwards on the broad path, descending this delectable heather moorland. Great views ahead lead to the Rombalds Moor skyline far beyond the Lothersdale valley. Within 300 yards a grooved, grassy path slants off to the left, its fading course offering a 130 yards detour down the slope to locate a small inscribed stone marked on the OS map. Robert Wilson died here in 1805, one of the guards who at this time still manned the beacon on a permanent basis: men of three surrounding parishes shared the duties.

The main path drops down to a wall, which it follows left along to a corner of the moor. At the stile at the bottom the moorland is left and a fieldside leads straight down to a short-lived enclosed green way, emerging onto the farm drive of Hewitts. This leads down to a back road. From the stile opposite descend the field to a stile and gate at the bottom, then turn sharp right with the wall. This leads an infallible course down to Lothersdale, with a wooded sidestream over to the left. Sleepy Lothersdale appears below, and at the bottom a firm track becomes enclosed to debouch via a farmyard onto the village street. The *Hare & Hounds* is handily placed just yards to the right.

Lothersdale is a highly attractive village strung along a quiet back road, and is very much off the beaten track. Its seclusion among folds of the hills did not prevent the arrival of the mill age, and the surviving chimney is indeed often all that can be seen of the village. The church stands high and isolated on the road to the east, while other features - including an old quarry from which prehistoric bones have been unearthed - are found further west.

The Hare & Hounds, Lothersdale

The Way turns left a few yards and heads down into the former mill yard opposite. Head straight on past numerous attractive cottages. Faced with Peel Terrace in front, turn sharp right on a short little way immediately after the mill building. This leads to the tall, square stone chimney that is such a Lothersdale landmark. From a little gate beneath it an inviting footpath runs downstream with Lothersdale Beck amid much greenery. This lovely section leads to a footbridge and ford by the small sewage works opposite. Don't cross, but continue a little further downstream, then before a gate veer right to a simple footbridge on a sidestream. From a wall-stile behind, a stiff pull to the right quickly eases out, climbing the field and remaining with the wall which runs left to the far corner. Here a leafy, enclosed snicket runs on to emerge onto a narrow back road (Mire Close Lane) alongside a house.

Go left just a few yards and take a stile by a gate on the right. Rise the few yards to a stile in the wall just above, and then climb the fieldside. Looking back, the impressive facade of the big house at Stone Gappe is unmistakable. Here, briefly, Charlotte Brontë was governess, and it became the Gateshead Hall of her world-famous novel *Jane Eyre*. Back in the village, initially only the mill chimney is visible, but is quickly joined by the church.

From the stile at the top continue up a much larger field, but before the top take a gap in the adjacent fence leading to a stone slab over a parallel trickle. Now slant up the field to the lone house of Greenburn Laithe, above. Pass to its right to find a stile in the top corner, just past the house. Joining its drive, this quickly leads out onto the road at Cowling Hill. With a graveyard in the trees opposite, this exposed farming hamlet was once an appreciably larger settlement astride a once important road. Though its pub is long gone, a surprising survivor is a Baptist church secreted among farm buildings.

Turn left, and at the junction take the narrow road (Shop Lane) on the right. The next stage beckons as the two monuments on Earl Crag are well seen above the straggling village of Cowling. **Descending, watch for a wall-stile on the left. From it descend two fields to the farm at Dairy House directly below. From a gate to its right descend a fieldside to a corner stile, and down again. When the colourful boundary hedge bends left, follow it down to a gate near the bottom. Here a track runs left to join an enclosed access track.** This is an old packhorse way known as Donkey Lane. **Turn right here, descending past a house at Gamsgill after which the rougher green way emerges into a sloping pasture above Gill Beck. The old way slants left down to a long, tall footbridge (Ridge Mill Bridge) over the beck.**

Across the bridge a good path turns upstream, but quickly finds itself tracing a different stream, Ickornshaw Beck, on the left. Quickly reaching isolated Wood House, fork left on a flagged path down to a footbridge on this beck. Across, a path climbs leafily away to join the bottom of a rough road alongside some houses on the edge of Cowling. Rise up here to meet the A6068 Keighley-Colne road. The bulk of the village is along to the right, though a shop and a chippy are found right on the route. This road was built at the beginning of the 19th century by a turnpike trust to link Airedale with Colne. Towards the end of the century there were plans for a railway to follow a similar course, but this never materialised and so Cowling continued to be served from Kildwick station on the Keighley-Skipton line.

Cowling is a windswept gritstone mill community, indeed a classic Pennine example. Its rows of dark terraces are strung along the length of the village, on or close to the main road over to Lancashire. The 19th century church stands aloof near the house where famous son Philip Snowden, early 20th century Chancellor of the Exchequer, was born. The *Bay Horse* is Cowling's centrally placed pub.

Turn right and cross the main road to Collinge Road, opposite. Head up this suburban street to the very end, where a snicket at the top left corner returns us to the fields. A part-flagged path climbs away, and the fainter path then slants left to a gap-stile at the top corner. This admits to the drive of Crag Side: go left onto Dick Lane. Rise a short way to a sharp bend, then take an old gate just above onto the foot of the moorland. A clear path rises away, bound unerringly for the monument. Though numerous old sunken ways are encountered, this same path slants straight up to the base of the rocks beneath the monument, the final section being a well engineered, abandoned green way. Simply clamber up through the modest rocks to gain the edge path, and advance the last few yards to Wainman's Pinnacle.

Dominating South Craven's skyline is the mile-long gritstone edge of Earl Crag. Atop it, a long half-mile apart, are its two permanent occupants. Built on solid rock, the pinnacle dates from the early 19th century and is better known as Cowling Pinnacle. The panorama is both extensive and absorbing: many of the more local features draw the eye beyond the rim of the outcrops, including Farnhill Moor, Pinhaw Beacon, Skipton Moor, Rombalds Moor and Airedale villages such as Cross Hills, Bradley and Kildwick. The promenade along the crest of Earl Crag to Lund's Tower is a local favourite, and worth undertaking if time permits. Known locally as Cowling Tower or Sutton Pinnacle, its grassy sward is set back from an old quarry. It boasts a spiral staircase up to a small platform from which to survey the exhilarating vista extending far into the Yorkshire Dales. The drop of the quarry exaggerates the airiness: not for the faint-hearted!

- On Earl Crag -
left:
Wainman's Pinnacle
right:
Lund's Tower

Resume by heading directly away from the edge, on a wallside path running from the wall corner to a parking area on Piper Lane at Stake Hill. Cross straight over to a gate from where a rougher path heads off, wallside again onto more rough moorland. The mighty landmark of the Hitching Stone beckons on the skyline just ahead. Beyond an intervening fence-stile the faint path drops towards a sluggish stream, with the Hitching Stone off-route just two minutes beyond.

The Hitching Stone is another local celebrity, though this time its gritstone sculpting is not the hand of man. This massive, isolated boulder offers an easy scramble onto its top, further improving an already magnificent panorama of TPW country. To the west rises Pendle Hill, with the Bowland moors to its right. Intriguingly, Yorkshire's famous Three Peaks each rise beyond a Lothersdale feature: Ingleborough is directly above Pinhaw's heather moorland, Whernside is behind Lothersdale's mill chimney, and Penyghent glides into place above the mansion of Stone Gappe. Sweeping further east, Rough Haw on Flasby Fell is directly behind Wainman's Pinnacle, then Buckden Pike and Great Whernside crown the head of Wharfedale, followed by Simon's Seat and Rombalds Moor.

The Hitching Stone

The route, meanwhile, crosses a makeshift stile where the wall gives way to a fence, rather nearer the Hitching Stone than the map suggests. From here quickly cross the stream of Hitching Stone Slack where it flows more decisively, and head off between marshy flats on the left and the base of a minor slope on the right. The Hitching Stone and a wall are further up above. When the stream bears off left (towards farm buildings further ahead), swing right to quickly encounter an old grassy trackway slanting down from the right. Merge into this and resume, remaining clear as it runs along the moor, now with the flat marshy basin of Quicken Hole on the right.

The path runs on to the end where a solid wall-stile awaits. This marks the modern boundary between North and West Yorkshire. **A thin path contours directly away through denser heather, and the stream on the right forms the deep-cut little valley of Slatesden Clough. Though the path fades, the way is obvious as the clough opens out: drop down to the end where a clearer path heads away through the mixed moorland vegetation of the New Allotment. With the stream still to the right, the trod runs on to reach a sturdy wall at the moor edge.**

The direct way goes left a few yards to a sturdy stile. From it cross the reedy pasture, and towards the end drop left to cross a stream there, then on to merge into a wallside track before the far corner. Here a gate gives access to a back road, Slippery Ford Lane. Turn right on here to meet the other option just past the farm at Far Slippery Ford.

The best route turns right with the wall, crossing the stream and rising with the wall to the corner where a stile awaits. A substantial shooting cabin on the edge of Keighley Moor is just ahead now, so continue on the vestiges of a grassy wallside trackway, crossing a marshy stream en route. Just round the corner from the cabin a stile by a gate sees us off the moor, and a grassy track heads down the pastures to become enclosed by walls before emerging onto a back road (Slippery Ford Lane) at Far Slippery Ford.

Turn right past Slitheroford Farm (Near Slippery Ford on maps) and down to Morkin Bridge. At the parking area turn right on a surfaced drive climbing to the house at Higher Intake. Shortly after starting out, the map shows the definitive path undertaking a short spell off to the right of this drive: it is, however, invisible on the ground, and seldom if ever used. Looking back downstream, this side valley is the local beauty spot of Newsholme Dean. **Above the house the road continues, back onto heather moorland with the bracken-flanked clough of Morkin Beck on the left.** A large isolated boulder is passed, a mere shadow of the Hitching Stone, but still finding Buckden Pike and Great Whernside in its view. **The heathery embankment of Keighley Moor Reservoir appears just a few minutes in front, and is quickly reached.** The reservoir was constructed as far back as the 1830s to supply water to local mills, and is known as the 'Big Dam'.

Surrounded by rolling heather, cross the embankment to a fork just beyond the end. Take the left branch, gliding gently down through the heather of Oakworth Moor and quickly becoming a firm

trackway, now with a wider Brontë skyline in front. The moorland horizon reaches from Ovenden Moor windfarm round to Crow Hill; Withins itself is rather easier to discern now. **An old wall comes in for company, and at a gateway in it a fork goes left. Keep on the thinner wallside way, however, soon reaching a wall junction as it swings left. Cross to the left side of the wall and resume along the moor edge, passing a small plantation and now earning big views ahead beyond Keighley to Rombalds Moor.**

A thin path leads on to a stile in the far corner. Looking back, it offers a last chance to see both of Earl Crag's monuments, the Pinnacle appearing alongside the Hitching Stone; on a good day Penyghent is still clear beyond. **Though the wall has temporarily vanished, maintain the line on a clearer path which runs to the next facing wall. Turn right on a broad track, rising over the brow and down through heather.** Haworth now appears ahead, to the left, with its solitary wind turbine more than evident: despite being a loner, it always appears far more jarring than the cluster of 23 at Ovenden Moor on the skyline beyond. Also in front is the village of Stanbury on its little ridge, with Lower Laithe and Ponden Reservoirs to either side.

Descend past an attractive little wood on the right, the track becoming firmer as it winds down through the heather colonised quarry site of Blue Stone Delph, to drop down onto a road at Hare Hill Edge. This finally marks the end of today's moorland. Go left for two minutes to the *Grouse Inn* at Hare Hill, above Oldfield. At exactly 1000ft/305m, the lounge of this popular pub makes a wonderfully sited (and comfortable!) viewpoint for the heart of Brontëland.

The Grouse Inn, Hare Hill

Continue down the road less than 200 yards beyond the pub, and take a gate on the right. Head down the wallside to emerge onto another road, Oldfield Lane. Go left a few yards to descend the sunken access road directly below. At a fork bear left to the side of Street Head Farm, and take a stile by a gate. From here there is a glimpse of attractive 18th century Laverock Hall back up to the left.

Continue slanting away from the house on a path down through a newly planted strip of woodland. The old way of Street Lane takes shape towards the bottom, and amid mature trees reaches a ladder-stile behind a sidestream. Immediately below is an attractive waterfall in a mini-ravine. **Advance a little further to a junction of ways. Ignoring the wooded clough on the right, opt for the stile just in front. Resume downhill at a more genteel angle, now as Hey Lane. A grassy section between old walls precedes a more hollowed descent onto a concrete access road. Cross straight over and resume down the field alongside the winding, sunken course of the old way. At the bottom corner pass through a gate to reach the river Worth.**

Long Bridge, River Worth

Turn upstream the few yards to the waiting Long Bridge. This shapely, stone arched footbridge is the focal point of our crossing of the Worth Valley by this old packhorse route. The narrow bridge hovers over a confluence of the river Worth and Sladen Beck, while also beneath it is a ford. The river Worth, sad to admit, begins life in Lancashire, emerging from the aptly named Watersheddles Reservoir to carve a deep course as a very modest stream, soon entering the better known Ponden Reservoir. Though harnessed to supply numerous mills in times past, it largely avoids human contact until skirting the edge of Keighley, after which it joins the Aire.

Cross the bridge and follow the path climbing away, initially above Sladen Beck, to a stile. The old way regains its sunken nature to climb between long crumbled walls, but part way up spoils itself and it is necessary to escape into the field edge. A ladder-stile at the top admits to the environs of a house, Lower Oldfield Farm.

Turn right up the old sunken drive to climb onto a road at the base of Penistone Hill. Go left on the footway, and at the edge of Haworth, just past a merging with the moor road, take an old kissing-gate on the right. From here a flagged path runs through the fields to enter the village alongside the Brontë Parsonage. This is now a museum of its illustrious former occupants - see overleaf. **Continue on the cobbled street past the former school (where Charlotte taught) and the church to emerge at the top of the main street, opposite the busy information centre.**

The Black Bull, Haworth

• *HAWORTH AND THE BRONTES*

In 1820 the Brontë family came to live in Haworth Parsonage, where all but one of them were to end their lives. The father, Rev. Patrick Brontë, had taken the curacy here after a spell at Thornton near Bradford: he was born in Ireland while his wife Maria hailed from Cornwall. Within five years she and the eldest daughters Maria and Elizabeth had passed on, leaving the four other children to reach adulthood. The three sisters departed on numerous occasions to spend largely unsuccessful spells as governesses in other parts of the country, while Branwell, the only brother, showed promise as an artist. His progress, however, soon halted, and after a spell as a railway clerk he returned home: stricken by illness he saw out his closing years as a regular of the *Black Bull*, adjacent to the church.

Haworth Parsonage

Meanwhile the sisters had also returned to the fold, but in their cases to begin their successful literary careers. When the first novels were published Emily and Anne had little time to enjoy any acclaim, for their deaths rapidly followed the demise of Branwell in 1848. Anne was buried in Scarborough, her works a little overshadowed by Emily's masterpiece *Wuthering Heights*. Charlotte's first published novel *Jane Eyre* was followed by further works. She even survived long enough to marry the Rev. Arthur Bell Nicholls in 1854, though tragically her flame was also to burn out the very next year. Thus Patrick Brontë was to outlive all his children, attaining the ripe old age of 84. The eldest, Charlotte, had not even reached middle age. What makes the story of the Brontë sisters so memorable is the nature of the background to their literary achievements, notably the intense hardship and adversity the family had faced, and more appreciably still the brooding mass of moorland beyond their home, where they sought and undoubtedly found untold inspiration.

Haworth ceased to be just another village in the 19th century when the fame of the Brontës spread, though it took until relatively recently to become a full blown tourist honeypot. Focal point is the cobbled main street, lined with shops and cafes unashamedly aimed at visitors, many of whom are not quite sure why they're here: some view the Brontë connection not unlike the 'Summer Wine' celebrity status of not so distant Holmfirth! Despite a parallel by-pass the poor old main street still resounds to the bustle of cars nudging gawping pedestrians into the gutters. The street climbs steeply to the parish church of St. Michael, surrounded by pubs. Only its tower remains from Patrick Brontë's time here, the rest having been rebuilt around 1880.

Haworth church

STAGE 5

HAWORTH TO ILKLEY

Distance: 14½ miles/23km

Map:
1:50,000
Landranger 104 - Leeds, Bradford & Harrogate
1:25,000
Explorer 27 - Lower Wharfedale & Washburn Valley
Pathfinder 682 - Bradford (replaced by an Explorer map in 2000, after which Outdoor Leisure 21 may also be needed)

A crossing from the Worth Valley to the Wharfe Valley, with the deep trough of Airedale encountered midway. This hugely colourful and absorbing country of steam trains, moorland, woodland and villages leads to the surprising charms of Bingley. In the company of the river Aire the town is skirted to find a re-union with the Leeds-Liverpool Canal, and one of the 'Seven Wonders' of the canal age. From here a short, stiff pull onto Rombalds Moor makes for a classic tramp to Ilkley, a bracing stride which concludes by descending its own world-famous moor.

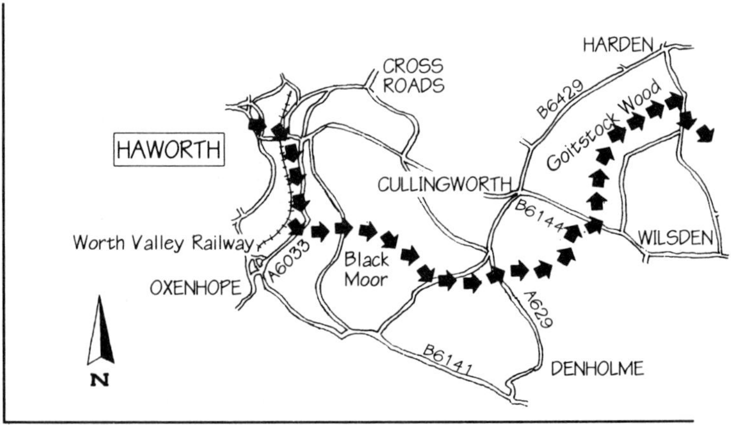

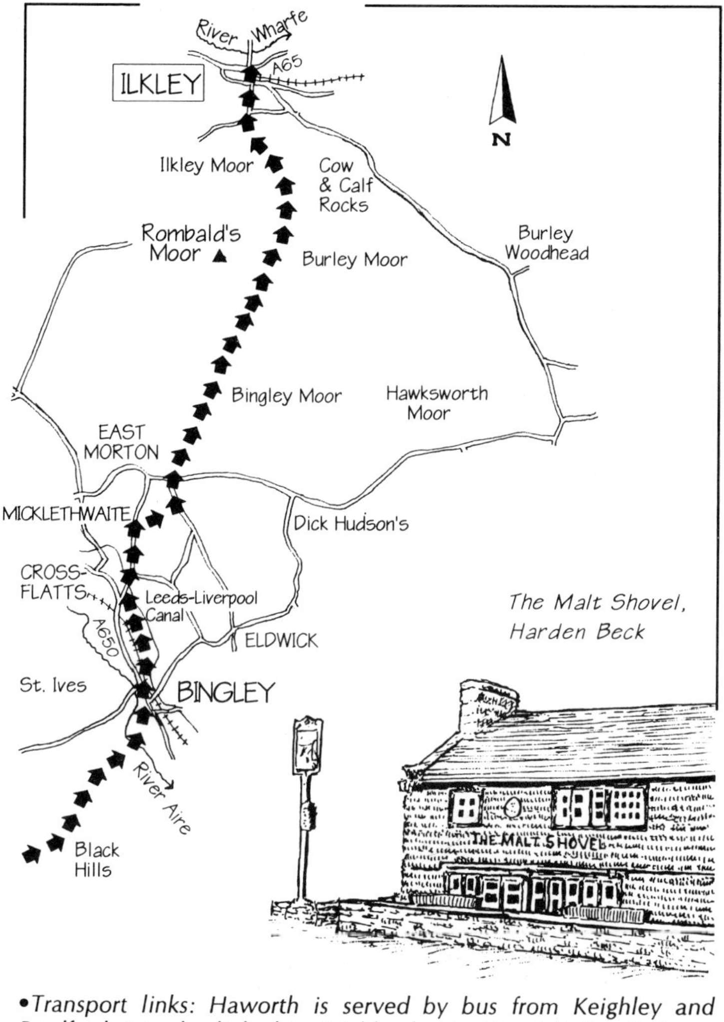

The Malt Shovel, Harden Beck

•Transport links: Haworth is served by bus from Keighley and Bradford. It is also linked to Keighley by the Worth Valley Railway. Keighley has trains to Bradford, Leeds, Skipton and beyond. Ilkley is served by bus from Keighley, Skipton, Bradford and Leeds, and has a train service to Leeds, Bradford and Shipley (for Keighley).

➡ **From the parish church descend the cobbled Main Street, and turn left off it down a steep little lane just yards before the *Fleece Inn*. At the bottom cross Rawdon Road (B6142) and descend the broad, stone setted Butt Lane alongside the park.** At the bottom a footbridge on the left crosses the railway line to Haworth station, home of the Keighley & Worth Valley Railway.

The 5-mile cul-de-sac line from Keighley was closed to passengers at the end of 1961, and six months later freight services were withdrawn. Already, however, enthusiasts had formed a preservation society, and in 1968 the line triumphantly re-opened at the dawn of independently preserved steam railways. Though short in length it is undoubtedly one of the finest and friendliest of such lines, with stations at Keighley, Ingrow, Damems, Oakworth, Haworth and Oxenhope. It has been a location for numerous film and television projects, but it was the making of the classic family film *The Railway Children* that earned the 'Worth Valley' a lasting fame. Another claim to fame is the operation of a buffet car purveying real beer, which has earned the KWVR a unique 'mobile' entry in the Good Beer Guide!

Main Street,
Haworth

Haworth Station, Keighley & Worth Valley Railway
The Leeds-Liverpool Canal near Crossflatts

The Old Hall at Micklethwaite
The Twelve Apostles Stone Circle, Ilkley Moor

At the bottom of Butt Lane turn right on Belle Isle Road, joining Bridgehouse Lane (B6142 again). Go left on the bridge over the railway (good view into the often busy yard) and bear immediately right on Brow Road. This immediately swings left to start climbing, but leave it just as quickly by taking a few steps up to a stile on the right, and a flagged path heads away. This path runs on the field bottom to join the long-drained course of a former mill-cut. Almost at once the bustle of Haworth is behind, and all is green. Over to the right the railway runs parallel across Bridgehouse Beck. Up above hover the flapping sails of the infamous Brow Moor wind turbine, the first in the area in 1992 and happily not yet joined by any colleagues.

Before long the path bridges the old cut and runs on with it to its demise, where the path forks. One branch drops down to a footbridge on the now adjacent beck, while ours runs straight ahead (featuring some old flagging) to an old house. Take a stile opposite and cross the field bottom to a gate into a garden. Pass along the front of the house, and at the gate as the drive heads away, the path turns down to the right to rejoin the beck. The next few yards, as far as a lovely stone arched bridge, are a 'permitted' path linking two rights of way. Don't be tempted to cross the bridge, but continue pleasantly upstream to a stile just before a simpler footbridge on the beck.

Just minutes further upstream is the village of Oxenhope. Terminus of the line, it has a rolling stock collection and refreshments. Oxenhope is a fine example of a Pennine mill community, though the principle features, i.e. the mills, have largely been replaced by housing!

Through the stile, leave the valley floor at another stile on the left, and climb the wallside to a stile onto the A6033 Keighley-Hebden Bridge road. Turn left for 150 yards to a bend, and take the bridleway up the far side of Royd House. This cart track climbs steeply to Upper Royd Barn, then swings right. From here there are big views over Oxenhope, in a basin amid steep hills rising to long moorland skylines. **Another drive is absorbed to rise onto Black Moor Road, and the first of the day's two notable climbs is complete.** On a clear day, look far to the north-west to see, above Oakworth Moor, the shapely outlines of both Ingleborough and Penyghent, some 28 miles distant.

Cross straight over Black Moor Road and head off along the roughly surfaced Cuckoo Park Lane. Ignoring any branches left this improves into a sandy track between heathery verges to emerge onto Black

Moor. Take the broad path slanting right to run a largely level course across this pocket heather moorland. There are big views left to Bingley, backed by the Rombalds Moor skyline. **Pass close to the edge of a big old quarry on the left before resuming on to a gate onto Trough Lane.** Straight in front is Sand Beds Farm, whose front bears a nice 1712 datestone, and with mullioned windows to front and rear.

Go briefly left on Trough Lane, and take the first right along a rough access road. After passing Copperas House on the right, take an old kissing-gate on the left just before the tiny stream (not as per map). Head away with the wall, and at the end another iron kissing-gate accesses an enclosed grassy way to reach Field Head Farm. Pass left and on through a private-looking gateway, to pass left of another house and out on a drive onto the busy A629 Keighley-Halifax road at Manywells Height. Just to the left is the large *Five Flags Hotel*, while Denholme is a long half-mile to the right. Another old mill village, it occupies a lofty situation midway between Keighley and Halifax.

Cross straight over to a gate left of a house, then descend to a stile from where a grassy path enters the beginnings of the side valley. The path crosses the tiny Milking Hole Beck (with a small aqueduct just upstream) and descends its bank, a glorious stroll into woodland beneath a noteworthy gritstone edge. Passing under a canopy of oaks the lovely path reaches a wall-stile, after which a tract of dense undergrowth leads out into the open. Here the path forks. The unofficial left branch keeps level to pick up the route across several pastures, but the right of way slants down to the right, through some gorse to then run downstream outside the wooded beck.

A path junction is reached at a bridge at the bottom. Bear left, rising back up the field to a stile at the top. Head away with a wall on the right, over which Hewenden Reservoir is fully seen now backed by Hewenden Viaduct. At the end an enclosed green way takes over, a pleasant ramble to run on past a small old quarry to join a farm track. Advance along to the farming hamlet of East Manywells.

After the short row on the right, double back a few yards down an access track, then turn left to descend the wallside away from the farm. Before the corner take a stile/gate in the wall and cross the next field corner to a stile in front of the wooded embankment of the old railway. Follow the wall around to pass under the penultimate arch, through a gate, and continue on. Trains on this old London & North

Eastern Railway line earned brief respite on the 18 arches of the viaduct during their long haul out of Keighley to Queensbury, where the celebrated Queensbury Triangle sent arms to Bradford and to Halifax. Both Cullingworth and Wilsden had village stations on either side of the viaduct's graceful curve, but sadly the line succumbed to closure in 1955. **As the wall swings away, cross the field to the left of a clump of trees, and from the stile follow the wall left around the fieldside to a stile onto the B6144 Haworth-Bradford road.**

Turn right down the welcome footway to Hewenden Bridge. As the footway ends take great care crossing the bridge. Thirty yards up the other side escape at a stile on the left and cross a small enclosure to a stile into undergrowth. Just over to the left is the former Hewenden Mill. **A path climbs to the top of the bank then heads along it, encountering brambles and nettles. At the end an open bank makes life easier, overlooking this wooded side valley before the final enclosure is crossed along the bottom of a replanted bank. A stile at the end admits onto a drive in front of the former Hallas Mill.** Sat deep in a wooded hole, it has undergone conversion into housing.

Advance a few yards up the drive to a bend, then take the path left, descending to pass the very side of the mill wall to the rear, then heading away downstream. Within a minute a junction is reached: turn left down to Hallas Bridge. Without crossing, take the path which sets off downstream on a delightful amble by the wooded bank of Harden Beck, deeply enclosed in the trees of Goit Stock Wood. After a small waterfall the main feature, Goit Stock Falls, is quickly reached, with a handrail assisting progress. This is a beautiful drop over a craggy wall into a deep bowl, the centrepiece of these glorious woodlands decorated by springtime bluebells.

Goit Stock Falls

This lovely walk resumes downstream to enter a caravan park. Keep straight on the road out of the site, where it bridges the beck. This now runs downstream through largely wooded surrounds. At a cattle-grid note the little falls on a bend above a former mill. **The road becomes Goit Stock Lane to emerge onto the Harden-Wilsden road at the bottom end of Harden village. Turn right to cross Harden Beck alongside the temptingly sited *Malt Shovel.***

Across the bridge quickly bear right off a dangerous section of Harden Lane and instead climb the sidelined Mill Hill Top. The main road is rejoined at a garden centre, whose car park makes safer going and may tempt use of its coffee shop. At the car park entrance cross the main road to a stile, and a slim path descends the field to cross tiny Wilsden Beck. The path runs across another field to a gap-stile to enter the wooded environs of Sandy Banks. Here a broad track is met. Don't join its zigzags but turn right up the wallside path, and when the track doubles back in, remain on the path which rises through an old gateway. At this fork climb left briefly, to resume on a higher level parallel path.

The path rises gently and runs a delightful course through the bracken floor of the woodland, with a wall on the left. One or two minor gritstone outcrops are encountered, along with some open views over the growing village of Wilsden. **At the end of the trees the path becomes enclosed, now almost on the edge of the village. Immediately through the gateway take a stile by a gate on the left, and stiles by gates lead along the same wallside through numerous fields to emerge onto Lee Lane.** Over to the left is the extensive St. Ives estate, with the plateau-top of Baildon Moor straight ahead. Between the two, half-left, is our goal of Rombalds Moor.

Go left 25 yards and take a stile/gate on the right. Head away with the wall, and in the corner a surprising enclosed way curves between the fields. Emerging, bear right to a gap-stile near the far end, and continue through the last field to a corner stile into the trees at Black Hills. A good path drops away through the wood, merging into a broader way to run to the right briefly. The path soon turns down the slope, a steeper and stonier sunken old way before again running right to a wall-stile out of the trees.

A thin path slants down the right side of this big pasture, through some low outcrops. A stile in the fence on the right sees us onto Shipley golf course. Bear left down through the course, a series of

enthusiastically white painted rocks aiding route finding. When these end, the way runs left across a fairway towards some houses. It leaves the course here to become enclosed as it bridges Harden Beck, to emerge alongside a converted mill onto Beckfoot Lane. Go right on this rough road to almost immediately reach Beck Foot. This is an idyllic location astride an old packhorse route, with an early 18th century arched bridge, a ford and some desirable cottages.

Don't cross the tempting bridge, but take a stile on the left to head on through the field. With the river Aire just below, and Myrtle Park opposite, this complete greenery makes it hard to believe we are on the edge of a town the size of Bingley. **Rising past a solitary house into trees, the path runs on and descends to a large open space before crossing the Aire by a substantial iron bridge.** Built to commemorate the Festival of Britain in 1951, it gives access to Myrtle Park. For the town centre go straight up through the park. **Our way turns left on the riverside walk to Ireland Bridge.** This pleasant stroll clings to the river, passing en route a picnic site, steps up to Market Street, and Ailsa Well. Identify this latter feature by a sign on a wall by a tasteful memorial: just through a gap and across a track, a flight of stone steps descend to a stone trough with water tinkling in, all hidden in greenery. The name Ailsa supposedly derives from Alice Hird, a local 'wise' woman.

Bingley is a bustling industrial town which has happily retained some of its older corners. In the spacious park is the Town Hall, which dates from Georgian times when it was the Myrtle Grove of the Busfeild family. Bingley received its first market charter in 1212, and the 18th century Market Hall was restored to this more central site as recently as 1984, along with the adjacent Butter Cross.

Old White Horse Inn, Bingley

A remarkable aspect of the town, already fully appreciated on the Trans-Pennine Way, is that the river Aire flowing parallel to its busy main street has repelled any development on its western bank: I have seen a kingfisher within five minutes walk of the overloaded main street. The Aire itself rises on lush pastures amid the dramatic limestone scenery of Malham, but has only a short time in the Yorkshire Dales before its journey through the broad valley past Skipton, Keighley and Bingley to Shipley. Beyond Leeds it runs through flat country to join the Ouse near Goole.

Meeting the B6429 Bingley-Harden road at Ireland Bridge on Millgate, pubs await at either end of it. Across the river stands the *Brown Cow Inn*, dispensing the prize-winning ales of Timothy Taylor's of Keighley. **The route crosses the road to the historic *Old White Horse Inn*. From it go briefly along the cobbled Old Main Street, and turn up a flagged path on the near side of the parish church.** All Saints church has 13th century origins, but most of the present structure is 15th century or later. **Cross the A650 Keighley-Bradford main road with care (traffic lights to the right if needed) and turn down the setts of the oddly named Treacle Cock Alley opposite.** On the left is a section of the old churchyard severed by the construction of the present road at the start of the 20th century.

The Five Rise Locks, Leeds-Liverpool Canal

The footway burrows beneath the Airedale railway and up as a snicket past allotments onto the Leeds-Liverpool Canal towpath at Three Rise Locks, so ending an ingenious passage through bustling Bingley. Though this encounter with the canal is as similarly brief as our earlier one at Salterforth, there is no shortage of interest. Sited in front of a large factory, this triple flight of locks would attract much greater attention were it not for the greater flight two minutes further. **The towpath leads left to quickly arrive at the celebrated Five Rise Locks.** Built in 1774, the five interlinking locks lift boats almost 60 feet up a watery staircase - a fascinating spectacle and a fine piece of engineering. These literally are staircase locks, in that the bottom gate of one is also the top gate of the lock below. Alongside is a shop/cafe.

Resuming, the towpath with its many moorings leads by the houses of Crossflatts to a swing bridge at Micklethwaite Wharf. Here vacate the canal and turn right up Micklethwaite Lane. We have views up the Aire Valley to Keighley, and back to the wooded slopes crowned by the rocks of the Druid's Altar. **Most of the traffic is lost at the first junction, and the footway leads pleasantly up into the straggling village of Micklethwaite. Continue straight up its full length.**

Micklethwaite is named from the Norse for 'big clearing'. En route we pass much of interest, first feature of note being the lower green, a charming spot quite recently restored. On one side sits the Manor House, dated 1601, its mullions and transoms largely unaffected by division into separate dwellings. Further along the main street seek out Micklethwaite Grange on the left, a tidy little dwelling dating from 1695. Legend suggests that Oliver Cromwell's men fired on the original grange with cannon positioned on the the Druid's Altar, across the valley. 17th and 18th century weavers' cottages feature amongst some attractive groupings, including High Fold by the phone box, opposite the Methodist chapel.

Above the upper, sloping green, the road leaves the village as Carr Lane. The neighbouring village of East Morton is well seen across the side valley of Morton Beck. **After the last houses on the left, but before the de-restriction sign, there are two adjacent gates on the right. From the upper one Hill Top Lane (a concrete drive) climbs away. Leave this well before the first house, on a quickly improving green way to the left. This old track steeply climbs a colourful, moor-like enclosure.** Extensive views look back to the sprawl of Keighley beneath a moorland skyline beyond the Worth Valley.

The Manor House, Micklethwaite

From a stile at the top left corner rise past a spring to the next wall-stile above. A messy corner is encountered here. Head away between wall and fence, quickly crossing a stile in the latter. As this offers no escape, double back a little to cross the morass before resuming up the field, slanting left to find a gap-stile at the top, well to the left of a gate. Turn left along Heights Lane, savouring the big view in the knowledge that all the day's work is done.

At the junction with Otley Road take a gate/stile just yards to the right, from where a grassy track shadows the wall enclosing the house on the right. This runs on to another gate/stile onto the open moor, and a superb Landrover track heads directly away over the vast spaciousness of Bingley Moor. This grand track through the heather is just one of several old moorland ways linking Bingley and Ilkley. **It is only vacated after a long half-mile, at a couple of stone posts. Here our path branches right to maintain the general line, and ultimately merges with a crumbling wall. It continues on to eventually arrive at a long-seen gap-stile in the sturdy ridge-wall crossing Rombalds Moor. Just through it is Ashlar Chair, the biggest boulder in the vicinity.** It serves as a boundary stone where the moors of Bingley, Morton, Ilkley and Burley meet, while by the wall to the right stands a more traditional boundary stone inscribed *ILB 1893*.

The path heads away for a couple more minutes to gain the true watershed. Over to the left stand the OS column and cairn on the summit of Rombalds Moor at 1319ft/402m. Over the crest a new panorama appears ahead, with Wharfedale curving exquisitely up to the left into the Yorkshire Dales National Park. The extensive view offers a host of features across Wharfedale, from distant mountain summits at the dalehead, down to Barden Moor, Chelker Reservoir with its four wind turbines, Simon's Seat, Beamsley Beacon, Round Hill (summit of the next stage), Lippersley Ridge, Norwood Edge (telecommunications mast), Menwith Hill (U.S. base 'golf balls' - a satellite tracking station), Almscliff Crag and Otley Chevin.

The path quickly drops past a couple of cairns to a junction with a cross-path. A few rocks stand to the left on this very minor edge at White Crag Moss. A short diversion to the Twelve Apostles stone circle is a tempting option here, see the panel overleaf. **The main route takes the barely discernible trod straight on, descending grassy moorland to meet the broad course of the much used Dick Hudson's path.** This is an historic trackway, having served the packhorse trade long before moorland tramping for pleasure was in vogue.

Through several examples of path restoration the way drops down across Ilkley Moor and around bracken-cloaked Gill Head. the path then undulates along to another crossroads before dropping left to arrive above the western rim of Ilkley Crags. This classic moment reveals a sweeping Wharfedale scene beyond the dramatic plunge to a tumble of boulders at the entrance to Rocky Valley, beneath our feet. Directly across the Wharfe is the exclusive settlement of Middleton, joined by Ilkley itself in the valley bottom. Also revealed is the unmistakable setting of White Wells just five minutes down the moor. By turning right here, the Cow & Calf Rocks can be quickly reached.

Ilkley Moor is a bracing tract of upland that stands for all that is best about the county of the broad acres. Gritstone edges and crags occur at various points on the moor, the major outcrops being around the Cow & Calf Rocks. Historically more significant are the innumerable evidences of early man, the moor being liberally dotted with stone circles, burial cairns, and the cup & ring markings that decorate many a boulder. Ilkley Moor is, in reality, just one part of the great sweep of Rombalds Moor, which it must share with a host of individually named moors. This upland ridge of Rombalds Moor stretches from Skipton to Guiseley, a high boundary between Aire and Wharfe.

• ***THE TWELVE APOSTLES***

For a five minute diversion to the Twelve Apostles stone circle, turn right on the level path at White Crag Moss to a cairned junction with the Dick Hudson's path just above the prominent boundary stoop of Lanshaw Lad. Inscribed with sets of initials and dates, the Lad still serves his purpose, as under his watchful eye a prominent line of yellow posts march up to delineate the division between Ilkley and Burley Moors.

Go right along the main path for just a couple of minutes to find the circle just off to the left. Presumed to be of Bronze Age origin like so many relics on the moor, its dozen stones are arranged into a neat circle 50 feet in diameter. Its well chosen site overlooks both Airedale and Wharfedale, and across to man's more intrusive ornaments on Menwith Hill. Return along the main path past Lanshaw Lad and descend this to be joined by the direct route.

The worn path drops steeply (look back to see the sheer main wall of Ilkley Crags, a haunt of rock climbers) and then runs on towards White Wells, where at a knoll with seats a right branch descends steps to the rear of the cottage. This humble cottage is a monument to Ilkley's great spa days. In the mid-19th century many large hydros were built for people to take of the therapeutic waters, but a century earlier Squire Middleton built White Wells as a bath-house to enable townsfolk to enjoy a dip in the pure moorland spring water.

White Wells was restored in the early 1970s and opened as a museum and visitor centre serving refreshments. Inside is a deep circular pool hollowed from the rock and fed by a cold mineral spring - though no longer available for a plunge! For half a century Ilkley flourished as the 'Malvern of the North', and the Victorians revelled in the 'healing' powers of its waters. By the turn of the century the fashion had passed, but by that time Ilkley was already firmly on the tourist map, and has continued to develop as such.

In front, a stepped path descends the final section of the moor to join Wells Road at the bottom. Drop down this into the town centre, preferably bearing left down Wells Promenade to enjoy the Victorian pathways of Well Gardens before emerging onto the main shopping thoroughfare, The Grove. The station and bus stops are just to the right, while the route continues straight down Brook Street to the crossroads by the parish church.

Ilkley is a thriving town just downstream from where the Wharfe leaves the Yorkshire Dales National Park. The river flows serenely by wooded banks just a stone's throw from the parish church of All Saints. It has a 500 year old tower and a 13th century doorway, but is best known for its Anglo-Saxon crosses: dating from the 9th century, the tallest and most important bears a figure of Christ, with four figures on the reverse. Seek out also a well-preserved effigy of Adam de Middleton, a 14th century knight. The church covers part of a Roman fort, built around 79AD and abandoned two centuries later. It was on the Romans' trans-Pennine road from Ribchester to Tadcaster, which here crossed another road from Manchester to Aldborough. Evidence is limited to a small section of preserved wall. Finally, also by the church, is the 16th century Manor House, now a museum of local historical interest. Shops, pubs and cafes line spacious streets decorated with great pride by a tapestry of floral colour, forever overlooked by the brooding mass of heather and gritstone that is Ilkley Moor.

The Old Bridge, Ilkley

STAGE 6

ILKLEY TO PATELEY BRIDGE

Distance: 16 miles/25½km

Map:
1:50,000
Landranger 99 - Northallerton & Ripon
Landranger 104 - Leeds, Bradford & Harrogate
1:25,000
Explorer 26 - Nidderdale
Explorer 27 - Lower Wharfedale & Washburn Valley

This is marginally the longest of the seven stages, though there is only one climb of note, and this comes at the very outset. Beyond Round Hill the Way enjoys an undulating mix of moorland, pastures, gritstone outcrops and woodland, often with sweeping views. The final approach to Nidderdale is quite superb. Almost from the outset this stage enters, and remains within, the Nidderdale Area of Outstanding Natural Beauty. Refreshment/supply opportunities are limited to a solitary pub midway through the day.

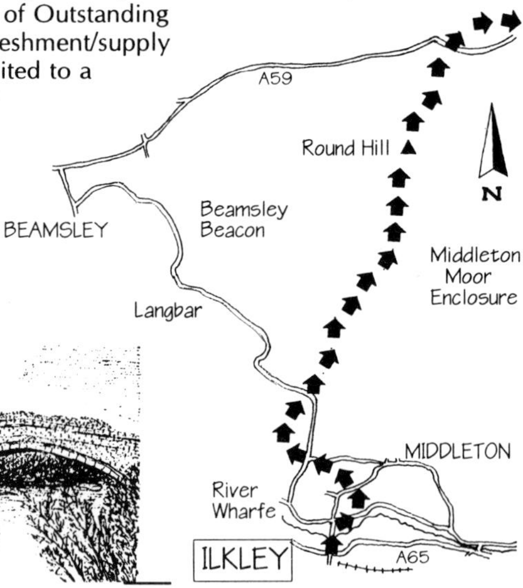

Pateley Bridge

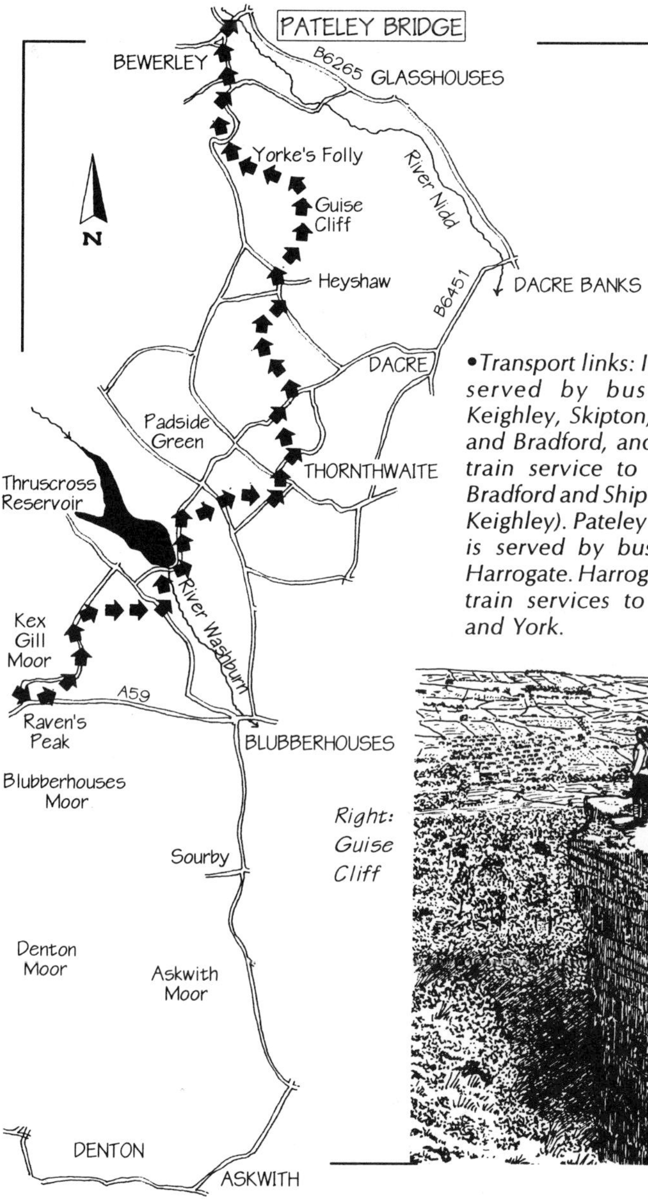

•Transport links: Ilkley is served by bus from Keighley, Skipton, Leeds and Bradford, and has a train service to Leeds, Bradford and Shipley (for Keighley). Pateley Bridge is served by bus from Harrogate. Harrogate has train services to Leeds and York.

Right: Guise Cliff

➡ **From the parish church resume by heading down New Brook Street to the river Wharfe.** The broad green spaces to the left are the townsfolk's memorial to the fallen of World War Two. Also here are the *Riverside Hotel*, rowing boats, and the graceful arch of the Old Bridge. Originally serving the packhorse trade, this was rebuilt after the great flood of 1673 that swept away many of the Wharfe's bridges. Happily it has long been left to be enjoyed by pedestrians, and a modern function is to send the Dales Way on its 80-odd mile course through the Dales to the Lake District. The river Wharfe rises in the heart of the Yorkshire Dales National Park, and brightens up countless villages before a more sedate flow through the characterful towns of Ilkley, Otley, Wetherby and Tadcaster to join the Ouse near Selby.

The modern road bridge was opened in 1904, replacing a ferry that supplemented the Old Bridge. **Cross the road and the bridge and descend to the riverbank to head downstream. Very soon the Wharfe is departed by going left with the hedge outside the rugby ground and up onto Denton Road. Cross straight over and along the driveway with the swimming pool on the right.** A nice day sees people everywhere, slurping ice cream and picnicking amongst the various sporting attractions. **Keep straight on up the grass, where at the end a path climbs a few steps through undergrowth to emerge onto Curly Hill, a suburban avenue.**

Go left just 30 yards, and across the road a path rises through rampant hollies into the delights of Middleton Woods. In springtime a carpet of bluebells makes it even harder to believe that planners could conceive of driving a by-pass through this beautiful and peaceful place. While there is quite a network of paths in this local authority owned woodland, our objective is to trace the public footpath rising towards the far side. **On meeting a broader path deeper in the wood, turn left. This runs on to cross a small stream, and ignoring a minor branch left, soon rises up its other side. A flight of stone steps lead up through less dense surrounds, soon bearing left at a level path junction just after a lesser branch left. This leads to another broader path: go left again, now with the edge of the wood in sight. This quickly leads to a stile out of the wood.**

At once there are grand views to the left, back over the town backed by the girth of its famous moor. **Slant up the field to a stile above, onto Hardings Lane. Go left to quickly reach a T-junction, where turn left a few yards to a narrow lane branching right.** Immediately below,

Crucifixion scene, Myddelton Lodge

the main entrance to Myddelton Lodge is graced by a beautiful crucifixion scene. Rebuilt around 1600 by William Middleton, the imposing gritstone building sports mullioned and transomed windows, and enjoying a broad outlook over the valley. The estate was in the hands of one of the oldest and most influential families in the county until it was passed to the Catholic church. The chapel was built in 1854, and for 50 years the folk of Ilkley climbed the hill to worship until a church was built in the town. Modern buildings alongside help fulfil its modern-day role as a pastoral centre of the Roman Catholic Diocese of Leeds, and various statues add to the charm of the grounds.

On the back lane, meanwhile, follow it sharp right at a bend, rising above the grounds of the lodge. After some cottages it swings sharp left, and here it is vacated. Immersed in woodland along to the left is Calvary, within the grounds of Myddelton Lodge. Created around 1850, intricately carved stones representing the Stations of the Cross line a path up to a grotto. This is a beautiful location where peace is exuded, and indeed needed.

The Way, meanwhile, takes the gate in front and straight up a cart track. Re-entering North Yorkshire, it climbs steadily outside a plantation to emerge into a field. While the track bears left, instead go through a gate to the right. Slant up the fieldside above the top of a wood to a gate back onto Hardings Lane at Primrose Hill. This junction of ways is an historic spot. The road climbing up is on the line of the Roman road of Walling Street from Ilkley to Boroughbridge, and the track known as Parks Lane traces its course onto the moor above.

With Windsover farm drive opposite, bear left up the dead-straight green track of Parks Lane. This leads onto a corner of Middleton Moor, with a big sweep of moorland ahead. Just yards to the right another old way (Hunger Hill) emerges onto the moor, and just to the left of its gate stands an inscribed milestone, complete with hands pointing the way to Skipton 6m, Ot(t)ley 7m, Ilkley 1m, and Rip(p)on 14m (yes, Ripon!). **Advance straight on the broad wallside track just as far as the wall corner ahead.** Though the Roman road departs, untracked, off to the right, our way remains a time-honoured route linking Ilkley with the Nidd Valley. **As the track forks at the wall corner, take the left branch directly over the moor, which these days carries modern transport in the form of shooting parties.**

Whilst apparently heading for complete wilderness, the track runs on to meet a wall to shadow it down to a wall-junction. Over it, green fields fall to March Ghyll Reservoir, while up to the left is Beamsley Beacon, from this angle merely a moorland bump. **At the junction the shooters' track continues up the wall-side onto the moor: shun this in favour of a ladder-stile into the grassy sheep pasture on the right. Follow the fence away, very briefly, then pass through a stile/gate back onto moorland. Another track is picked up, and virtually at once it fords the little stream of Loftshaw Gill.**

Almost immediately after, two ancient ways fork. Take the less obvious left branch which rises to the right of a line of shooting butts. This same grassy track rises unfailingly and delightfully up Middleton Moor Enclosure, interrupted only at a fence-gate, after which heather replaces bracken. In time the wall we left at the bottom returns, parallel with another series of butts: the climbing is all but done now. Looking back, there is a fine skyline of Otley Chevin and Rombalds Moor beyond our own rolling moorland.

Boundary stone, Round Hill

Passing the butts, the track dwindles to a single trod, largely as a splendid grassy causeway through the heather. The bridleway strictly passes through a gateway in the old wall, but

Springtime in Middleton Woods, near Ilkley
The High Street, Pateley Bridge

A rare quiet day at Brimham Rocks
The Cistercian splendour of Fountains Abbey

a more visible trod runs straight on to the watershed wall on Round Hill, just ahead. At the wall junction, a boundary stone inscribed *MM 1734* is found in a setting that demands a fair pause. The actual summit of Round Hill (formerly better known as Black Fell) is marked by a cairn to which a short trod runs out behind the junction. At 1342ft/409m this is the highest point of this great swathe of moorland between the Wharfe and the Washburn.

The panorama opens out to the north and west now, over Beamsley Beacon to the northern scarp of Barden Moor. Much more Dales country is beyond, with Great Whernside's mighty whaleback far up Wharfedale. To the west, Flasby Fell leads past Skipton to a distant Pendle Hill and to Boulsworth Hill; moorlands to the south are identified by man's adornments, including Emley Moor TV mast, Rombalds Moor with its twin radio masts, and to their right, beyond, Ovenden Moor windfarm.

The main route goes left on the wallside path, just a hundred or so yards down to a cairn at a pronounced bend at Little Gate. This is the closest the Way comes to a National Park, the Yorkshire Dales boundary here being touched at its south-eastern corner. **While a path runs out left towards Beamsley Beacon, ours passes through a gateway in the wall and heads clearly off north-north-east across the western reaches of Blubberhouses Moor (not the Landrover track which keeps nearer the wall).**

A new scene quickly greets the eye, man's hand again evident in the form of Blubberhouses Quarry, the A59 Skipton-Harrogate road, and the 'golf balls' at Menwith Hill; on a clear day the Hambleton Hills form a long skyline across the Vale of York. Nevertheless, for a short while we also retain the Wharfedale views, framed as ever by Barden Moor and Simon's Seat. **A pronounced descent soon follows, then skirting the marshy Mossy Sikes to a stream crossing and gate onto the main road.**

Cross with care and take a gate opposite, where an abandoned section of Kex Gill Road heads away as a bridleway. Tramp this in peace to a junction at the end. Note that an alternative path leaves this at a stile before the end, offering a more direct route to Turnwath Bridge by way of Kex Gill Moor. It is, however, rough and pathless. **While one could advance straight on past the quarry site, for greater interest turn right to rejoin the main road at Raven's Peak.**

Just a minute along the verge to the left a splendid green path swings off to the left, running along through bracken to the crest of a gritstone crag. It contours on past a spring to a second, more impressive cliff. Appealing to rock climbers, who know it as Dovestone, it is also a landmark for travellers on the road below. Its flat top makes an ideal place for a break. Note the shoring-up of the road opposite to counteract subsidence: this section is notorious for disruption by winter snowfalls. **A trod runs on past them, maintaining height to veer left, rejoining Kex Gill Road just short of a sharp bend.**

Continue along the road (now as Street Lane), which descends to cross a beck at Turnwath Bridge. Just up the other side take a stile on the right just 60 yards beyond a cattle-grid. A green track heads away, shadowing the wall on the left. Whilst in its company, note the enticing outcrops of Brandrith Crags on the Hall Moor skyline to the right. **The track runs a good course through several pastures gone to seed, in time crossing to the wall's other side on the open country of Burnt Hill. At a wall junction further along, ignore the improving green track heading on, and go by crumbling walls to a gate/stile into a small field.** Fewston Reservoir is now in view straight down the Washburn Valley. While the river Washburn flows into the Wharfe on the edge of busy Otley, its winding miles from its moorland beginnings are in stark contrast. Here, water rules the landscape, a chain of reservoirs harnessing the river and its gathering grounds in a manner that has largely blended well into the scene.

At Raven's Peak, Kex Gill

Cross to the bottom corner of the field to enter an abandoned green way down towards Redshaw Hall. Many years derelict, this fine old farmhouse has been restored in very recent times. **Without entering its yard, take a stile in the facing wall below, and descend the fieldside onto a back road. Go left no more than 20 yards to find a stile in the wall below. A thin path drops away, then slants down to the right to an old stile into a larch plantation. A path then drops down onto a surfaced access road. Turn left along this, with the concrete dam of Thruscross Reservoir looming large, ahead.**

When the surface ends at a turning area, take a path climbing steeply through bracken and trees on the left, to emerge by the top of the dam. With a car park just up to the left, go straight ahead to join the road at the end of the dam. Thruscross Reservoir is the fourth and (hopefully!) final piece in the string of Washburn lakes, having only been completed as recently as 1966. Sacrificed in the process was the hamlet of West End, which has since returned to daylight in times of drought.

Cross to the far end and remain on the road. The waters are currently hidden by the inevitable barrier of trees. As the road climbs away the reservoir returns to view, backed by a moorland skyline. **At the top of the steep pull above the couple of houses, a choice awaits.** Keep straight on for the quickest way to the bar of the *Stone House Inn*, at the crossroads just ahead. This isolated hostelry presides over a windswept crossroads at 918ft/280m, and is the only pub on this section from Ilkley to Pateley Bridge. Emerging from the pub door, turn left a short way to rejoin the direct route at a gate/stile on the left.

Just opposite the highest house, the Way proper takes a gate on the right to slant left down the stony pasture to the left-hand wall corner. Through a gateway in a fence bear left across a tussocky pasture, locating a makeshift stile onto Greenhow Hill Road. Cross straight over to a better stile by a gate and head away with the wall. From the gate at the end bear right to the far corner of this rougher pasture, to find a stile just yards from the wall corner. This offers a fine view ahead over Nidderdale, while just over to the left is the characterful outcrop of Calf Crags - a little gritstone gem. **The route, meanwhile, slants down this pocket of moorland to a gate at the bottom corner. From it a walled track heads away to join a back lane, which descends to a T-junction at the hamlet of Thornthwaite.** An indecipherable old milestone stands on this grassy triangle.

Go left the short distance to a fork, then bear right down Church Lane. Note that although the map suggests a short-cut path down a short driveway on the right before the road forks, this is not strictly usable as the first few yards are not a public path (the path actually comes in from a stile on the right, not down from the road). **The narrow road curves down past Church Lane Farm to reach Thornthwaite's parish church.**

The isolated church of St. Saviour is a modest place of worship with a lovely interior. Its stained glass includes the fine pair of heroines Florence Nightingale and Grace Darling. It was built in 1810 on the site of a much older chapel in the Forest of Knaresborough, and features a single bell-cote dated 1863. In the porch stands a stone salvaged from the church of the Holy Trinity at Thruscross, where in October 1965 the last service was held before the valley was flooded.

Thornthwaite packhorse bridge

Resume down the lane past a sturdy horse chestnut tree to approach Thornthwaite packhorse bridge, to which a stile gives access. This gem of a bridge survives in a peaceful wooded setting astride Padside Beck. It appears almost miniature, yet survives on this ancient route, a former monks' way leading to Fountains Abbey.

Across the bridge, turn left to a wall-stile and maintain this direction, upstream but separated by the wall. Through several intervening stiles the way savours increasingly colourful terrain to enter denser woodland. Remain close to the right-hand wall, ultimately emerging

via a stile onto the Thruscross-Dacre road. Turn up this for a few minutes, and at the bend at the top, take a gate on the left from where a walled green track heads away. Broad views look back over this side valley of Padside Beck. **At Old Fold Crag the bridleway passes beneath a massive boulder on which a holly has found a home, then runs through open country between the scattered rocks of Long Ridge Crags.**

Becoming enclosed again the track drops down to approach the tree-lined Black Sike. Bridging this, the fainter way crosses a field centre to Banger House Farm. Approaching the gate and stile by the farmhouse, don't enter but turn sharp right to follow the wall to a gate in the corner. With Grange House ahead, bear right to a sturdy wall-stile, then head away briefly with a wall on the left. Cross before the corner where a short fence takes over, and a well-placed slab footbridge crosses the mire from where rise up the field to Grange House.

Turn right along the drive. Note to the left, beyond the farm, an isolated building that is a former Methodist chapel; a partly uncovered stone causey runs to it. **The drive, meanwhile, climbs through a field to join a road, but the actual path leaves it on approaching a barn at the top. From a stile behind the barn, it crosses the grounds of a house and passes between two buildings to a stile onto Dike Lane.**

Turn left up this quiet road, past Woodmanwray Lane branching left, and just beyond is the branch of Heyshaw Road. Advance just a few yards further up Dike Lane and take a stile on the right. Cross to the far corner of the field to find a stile in the right-hand wall, 50 yards before the end. From here maintain the line towards the next corner, and take a stile a few yards left of the gate. Now simply cross towards the clump of trees sheltering the buildings at Hill Top, to join a rough road just in front of them. Turn left on this to a gate onto a corner of the open moor, with the large mast above Guise Cliff waiting ahead. There are big views across the main valley to the side valley of Fell Beck beneath Brimham Rocks.

The track runs on beneath the heather reclaimed spoil of old quarries, then above the isolated house at Hood Gap to arrive at a path crossroads in front of the mast. Pass around the top side of its perimeter fence, beyond which a path heads away alongside a wall. Soon this crumbles away and the path finds itself above the exposed

beginnings of Guise Cliff. Note that the map shows the invisible right of way to be further inland, across the moor. Be warned: children and vertigo sufferers should not be near the edge, not only for the all too obvious sheer drop (which falls 100 feet at its peak) but because there are also some mischievous crevices. Revealed is a glorious panorama of the dale, much of it seen as on a map beyond the magnificent rock architecture. The blanket of woodland below is so complete as to largely hide the still waters of the oval Guisecliff Tarn in its midst. Higher up Nidderdale, Pateley Bridge leads the eye to Gouthwaite Reservoir and a distant moorland skyline.

The path runs unerringly left along the crest, with tempting branches seeking out even more exposed situations. Soon a wall comes in to halt the fun, and the path runs on the moor edge to the waiting towers of Yorke's Folly, reached by way of a ladder-stile re-crossing the wall. Highly prominent in many a Nidderdale scene, it was built 200 years ago by a member of the Yorke family to provide local employment. Supposed to resemble a Rhineland ruin, it probably does more so since one of the three original towers succumbed to a storm in 1893, making redundant its local name of Three Stoops. **Beyond, the path descends gradually but quickly to the road on Nought Bank.**

Yorke's Folly

From the kissing-gate opposite, a path runs down more moorland to a stile, then down into the top of Skrikes Wood, an enchanting nature reserve. Bearing down to the right into the trees, it quickly reaches the edge of the wood. Here leave by a wall-stile, and descend the large field with

grand views to join the road again at another stile. Go left down this to run along to Turner Bridge, crossing it to enter Bewerley. On the right is Bewerley Grange Chapel, built as a grange of Fountains by Marmaduke Huby, Abbot from 1494-1526. Sympathetically restored in 1965, it stands in peaceful grounds a world apart from Pateley just over the river. **Keep right at the end of the village to quickly enter Pateley Bridge, appropriately by way of the bridge on the river Nidd.**

Bewerley Grange Chapel

Immediately before the bridge are two riverside parks. On the left is the public recreation area, while on the right is Bewerley Park, which hosts the prestigious Nidderdale Show (a continuation of the Feast of St. Mary, dating from 1320) in September. The Nidd itself springs to life more than 2000ft up on the slopes of Great Whernside, to be incarcerated in three reservoirs and also enjoy a subterranean course before reaching Pateley. Downstream it flows more sedately through the Nidd Valley, adding colour to the town of Knaresborough before meandering to join the river Ouse a few miles short of the city of York.

Pateley Bridge is a busy little town, the undisputed capital of Nidderdale. It draws from far and wide: to Nidderdale folk it is the hub of dale life, to visitors from further afield, the first stop. It is literally the key to the upper dale, for all intent on exploring these finest, wilder reaches will pass through here first. Within the town itself are several pubs and cafes, an information centre, innumerable shops hidden down inviting narrow alleys, and the award-winning Nidderdale Museum. On display here are over 4000 items of life gone by. Unfortunately most of Pateley's industry comes within its scope, for at one time railways, mining and quarrying could be added to the more durable farming.

STAGE 7

PATELEY BRIDGE TO RIPON

Distance: 14½ miles/23km

Map:
1:50,000
Landranger 99 - Northallerton & Ripon
1:25,000
Explorer 26 - Nidderdale (to be re-numbered)

• *Transport links: Both Pateley Bridge and Ripon have bus services to Harrogate. Ripon-Harrogate buses continue to Leeds. Harrogate is also linked by rail to Leeds and York.*

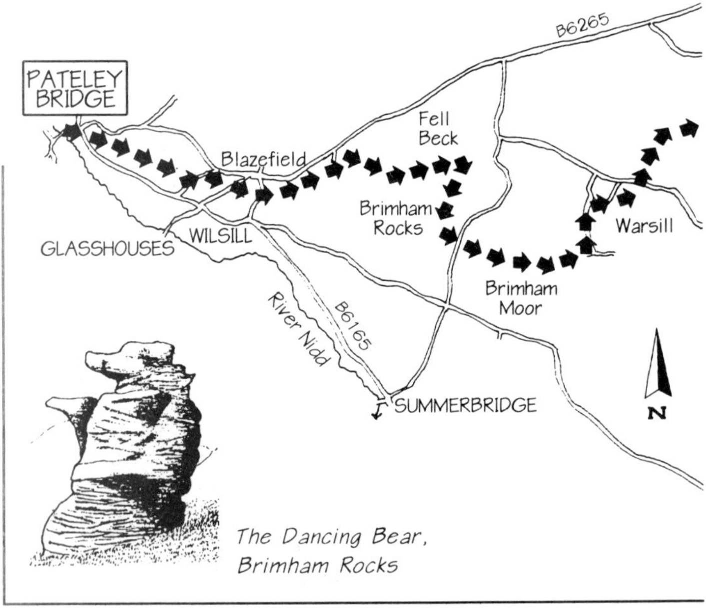

The Dancing Bear, Brimham Rocks

Despite its appreciable mileage this final day has a 'winding down' feel to it, as the lingering bastions of Pennine country at Brimham Rocks usher us out of Nidderdale and send the Way off to conclude through park-like surrounds. National Trust properties feature strongly, for in addition to Brimham, Fountains Abbey and Studley Royal estate are unforgettable obstacles to reaching Ripon. This stage remains within the Nidderdale Area of Outstanding Natural Beauty to within a couple of miles of the walk's conclusion.

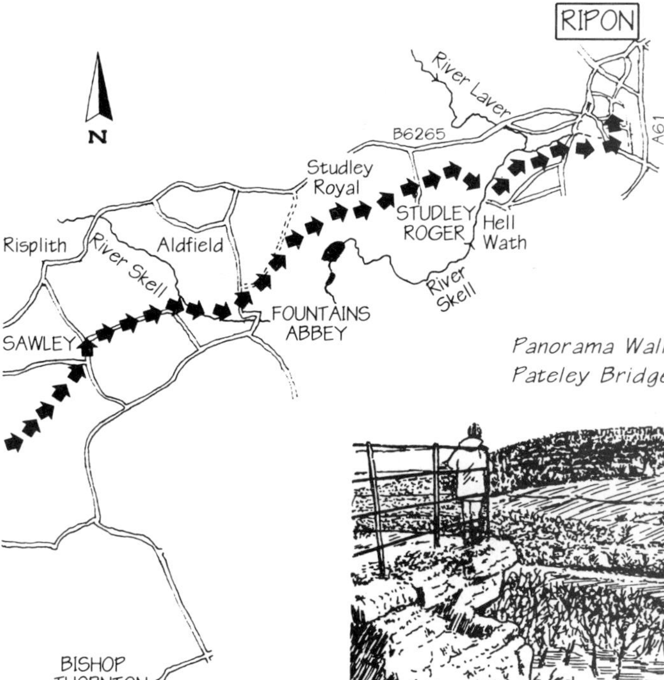

Panorama Walk, Pateley Bridge

➡ **From the bridge at the foot of the High Street head up the main thoroughfare, swinging right at the top (Ripon Road) to quickly level out. After 150 yards or so an urban footpath sign points up a flight of steps to the start of the Panorama Walk. A steep, enclosed tarmac path climbs past an inscribed stone tablet above a well.** Our route coincides with the Nidderdale Way for three miles, as far as the crossing of Fell Beck.

Early views look back up-dale over the church tower, with Great Whernside already slotting in on the horizon. Beyond the entrance to the cemetery a snicket runs along to the old church, offering en route wide views over Bewerley Moor and Gouthwaite Reservoir beyond the gravestones. Embowered in trees in high altitude seclusion, the roofless church of St. Mary dates from the 13th century. It was replaced by the parish church of St. Cuthbert in the 19th century, and saved from complete ruin as a sister's memorial to her brother in 1906.

The old church of St. Mary, Pateley Bridge

On the main route the gradient soon eases and the way remains surfaced, enabling the views to be appreciated effortlessly. Part way along, an iron gate admits to a traditional viewing station on a craggy knoll. Probably the finest feature is the prospect of Guise Cliff directly across the valley, with Yorke's Folly silhouetted (yesterday's final miles). **On reaching the tidy hamlet of Knott, the track widens into a road. As it swings right to descend to the main road, keep straight on a cart track to the left. After an isolated house it runs on as a tightly enclosed footway. At a fork at the end drop right, again pleasantly leafy to run out onto the B6265 Pateley Bridge-Ripon road.**

Turn up this a short way. An old milestone is passed advising the distances to Skipton, Pateley and Ripon. **At the first opportunity turn right along a private road past the houses of Blazefield. At the end the rough road drops onto a back road. Turn up this to quickly level out, enjoying superb views downdale. As the road turns sharp left to a T-junction, instead keep straight on another enclosed footway to meet another road. This time turn downhill, just as far as a hairpin bend. Here take an old driveway heading off left. The track ends at a gateway above an abandoned modern house, and a footpath takes over. This maintains the slightly rising course beneath an increasingly colourful bank of heather and outcrops, running on to emerge onto a junction of ways above a farm at White Houses.**

Go straight across on a cart track opposite. The side valley of Fell Beck leads the eye over wonderfully wooded country to the impending Brimham Rocks skyline. **Through much varied vegetation the way narrows to a path to approach a short terrace of houses. Turn down the nearside of the garden to a stile, and descend the fieldside. From a stile at the tapering field bottom go left down the wallside sunken way, crossing the wall at a gateway and slanting down to join an access track. Go left on this the short way to a junction where two such ways meet a rough road. Turn right down this a few yards, then go left to a footbridge and ford on Fell Beck.**

Across, the path forks: while the Nidderdale Way goes right, instead take the stile on the left and turn upstream, a faint track rising outside the wooded environs of the beck. Note that the map incorrectly shows this pasture as being wooded. Climbing away, ignore two stiles into the trees and take the gate at the top. The track rises to another gate then fades. Simply follow the fieldside up to a stile at the top corner. After a few enclosed yards, rise with the right-hand

wall to a stile. Now cross the field to meet the driveway at Brimham Rocks House (High North Pasture Farm on the map). Keep right of all the buildings and head away on the drive.

With Brimham Rocks just above, the track runs on into trees. On emerging from the denser patch, with an open field to the left, advance a little further to a National Trust boundary sign. Now in the Trust's open country of Brimham Moor, double back right on an inviting green path. This curves up beneath the first outcrops, and on through heather to rise to the start of the Rocks proper. Here the end of a well used 'loop' path is met. Preferably take the right branch which runs through a parade of wonderful outcrops, passing several natural viewing platforms overlooking Nidderdale. Some particularly notable monoliths include the Yoke of Oxen, the Idol Rock and the Dancing Bear. Just past this rock Brimham House is reached.

Brimham Rocks are the pride of Nidderdale, a startling collection of gritstone outcrops weathered into innumerable weirdly sculpted shapes. Brimham House is the focal point of the estate. Formerly the Rocks House, it was built in 1792 by Lord Grantley for his moor keeper, and as part of the estate it was left to the National Trust in 1970. The house now serves as a shop and information point, with all the usual National Trust aromas. Refreshments and toilets are also in evidence.

The Druid's Writing Desk, Brimham

From here the heart of the Rocks await. The direct route is the broad carriageway heading away to the car park, but infinitely better is the broad pathway to its right, which takes a meandering course through the myriad boulders above the western scarp. A hundred offshoots seek out the hidden delights in this natural wonderland, where the activities of rock climbers and the extensive Nidderdale views add even further interest. **At the end the path enters the car park. Follow the short drive out onto the road crossing Brimham Moor, and go right for just 100 yards.**

Here the Nidderdale Way is rejoined for less than a mile, by turning off left on an inviting path striding out through rolling heather. Though of modest extent, this National Trust land appears much greater as it sweeps away to the left. Further back, some of the famous rocks still rise from bracken and wooded surrounds. **At the end a gate/stile in a boundary wall see us off Brimham Moor, and a similarly nice path heads away. This emerges onto a farm drive beneath Riva Hill, and runs on to a corner. Now the Nidderdale Way takes the track to the right, while our chosen route remains on the concrete farm drive which drops down to the left between walls.** Ahead is an archetypal rolling English landscape, with a wealth of trees bounding fields and pockets of woodland. **Through trees in the bottom it rises as the narrow Chapel Lane. Passing an old Methodist chapel with a Victorian postbox affixed, we reach a junction with the identical cul-de-sac of Warren Lane in this scattered parish of Warsill.**

Turn left, rising gently to reach Middle South Farm on the right. The easiest option is to continue to a junction, then turn right. A footpath, however, cuts a tiny corner by doubling back right along the second of parallel drives, to Middle Farm. At the entrance to the yard, take a gate on the left and head along the field-edge to the far corner, where undergrowth entirely obscures the gate with only a crumbling wall to the left. **Advance along the road past South East Farm on the right.** A cottage on the left is overlooked, somewhat bizarrely, by a stray from Brimham, a fine adornment to any garden.

The road then bends left to arrive at a caravan site at Warren Forest. Immediately before it turn into the paddock on the right, and drop down with the wall outside the rear of the site buildings. Simply remain with the wallside outside the wooded site. Pass through several gates and along to a gate at the end back onto a road. Go right just a field's-length and take a gate/stile on the left, to follow the

fence along to a plantation corner. A bridle-gate sees us resume outside the trees, tracing the wall along to a drive just in front of Warsill Hall Farm.

Without entering the farm take a gate on the left, and after 30 yards leave the track by a wall-stile on the right. Cross to the far corner of the field, and from the right-hand of two gates, descend the wallside on the right to a gateway. Continue straight down to a bridle-gate into the trees of Booth Wood. A splendid old sunken way slants gently down below a collapsed wall, a dark interlude even on a sunny day. It descends into a clearing and onto a broad forest track to cross the ancient and remarkably overgrown Butterton Bridge.

Across the bridge, join a firmer forest road. With no sign of a path in front, go left 60 yards to a junction, where a track climbs back to the right. Double back up this to leave the wood at a bridle-gate. With a spring emerging into a stone trough on the left, bear right up this field enclosed by plantations, aiming for the far end of the row of trees above. A track forms, leading to a stile onto the head of well named Green Lane. After just 80 yards, use a stile on the left and cross to the far corner of the field, passing Lacon Cross. This wayside cross on its solid base is hollowed at the top, and dates from monastic times when it was astride a route west from Fountains Abbey towards Nidderdale.

Lacon Cross

From the stile descend the fieldside past a scattering of stones, embracing some pleasant rolling terrain. Just below is Lacon Hall, while the Hambleton Hills form the horizon far across the Vale of Mowbray. The faint path shows signs of causeying, being distinctly raised in parts and clearly of some age. After Butterton Bridge and Lacon Cross, this is yet more evidence of this centuries-old route. **At the bottom the path crosses a stile to enter the environs of Lacon Hall, passing through the garden onto the drive between the buildings.** On the right is the hall itself, its mullioned windows part of an attractive frontage largely hidden to the south. Dating from the 16th century, it replaced an earlier timber hall of the once influential Lacon family.

Follow the drive out just as far as a cattle-grid. Now bear left off the drive, rising gently to the very far end of the field, where a stile sits in a holly hedge. Advance across the next field, merging with the hedge on the right to reach a gate/stile at the far end. Sawley is just ahead now, and cross one last field to a stile at the far end to emerge onto a junction with Sawley Moor Lane. Go straight ahead to enter the village.

Sawley is a small, outwardly affluent village in the estate country west of Fountains Abbey. The modest church of St. Michael & All Angels dates from 1879 but is on the site of a chapel built by Archbishop Huby of Fountains. The bell remains in situ atop a former schoolhouse, a fairly recent casualty at the top end of the village green. Also centrally placed is the *Sawley Arms*.

Turn right opposite the pub and head out of the village along Low Gate Lane, which is followed for rather less than a mile. A feature of interest on the left is the tiny old house of Hogg Hall, featuring arch-headed mullioned windows; alongside is a fine range of farm buildings with vernacular red pantile roofs. **As the lane swings to the right a stile sends a path into the trees. This descends to the river Skell where this modest stream is crossed on an attractive stone-arched footbridge. Joining an estate track turn downstream on it, startling pheasants aplenty. The woodland is left at a gate alongside a substantial stone arched bridge, and the track quickly rises onto a road.** Just ahead is a glimpse of Fountains Hall and the upper section of Huby's Tower, at the Abbey. **Here a choice awaits. The 'official' line of the Way turns left, while the recommended route turns right.**

If this makes little sense, read on. The true Way rightly keeps to (free!) public paths that are always open. Although a nice walk, it must be conceded as inferior to the stupendous delights of Fountains Abbey and Studley Royal. The routes rejoin at St. Mary's church in the deer park at the other end of the grounds, and the direct route continues after a two-page interlude for the 'Fountains option'.

• ***FOUNTAINS ABBEY***

Fountains Abbey and Studley Royal bear the prestige designation of World Heritage Site. The best route takes in the full range of Fountains Abbey and Studley Royal, and is memorable. This is a National Trust property with an admission charge for non members, but worth every penny. The abbey is open daily from 10am, except Christmas Eve, Christmas Day, and Fridays in January, November and December. It closes at 7pm Apr-Sep, 5pm Oct-Mar; last admission is one hour before closing.

Turn right along the road to Fountains Bridge, where enter the grounds and pay your money by the West Entrance (this was the main entrance until the modern visitor centre was opened). First feature of interest, and a major one in its own right, is Fountains Hall. With its intricate facade the magnificent hall was completed in 1611, much of the stone coming from the abbey abandoned only decades earlier. Last private owners were the Vyner family, descendants of the Aislabies - mentioned shortly - and much evidence of their presence is found here, including a particularly touching memorial in the hall entrance stairway. Continuing, a new path leads up from the carriageway to the visitor centre.

Back on the main carriageway, set forth to explore the delights of this staggeringly beautiful ruin, the most extensive Cistercian remains in England. Fountains Abbey was founded in 1132 by a group of dissatisfied Benedictine monks from St. Mary's Abbey in York: seeking a stricter routine they turned to the French Cistercian order. Though it would have been a much wilder place then, the setting they chose is matched only by perhaps Bolton and Rievaulx.

Built largely between the mid 12th and 13th centuries, this was one of the most important religious houses. Whilst their granges occupied much of nearby Nidderdale, their possessions stretched to the Cumberland fells. Dairy farming, lead mining and other industry also came within their scope: many peoples' lives revolved around the abbey. Perhaps the abbey's finest feature is the enormous 300ft long west range (more commonly known as the cellarium), its vault arched roof being quite stunning. Most impressive, however, is the 180ft high tower, a 16th century addition built by Abbot Marmaduke Huby: it remained incomplete at the Dissolution.

Rejoining the main carriageway, this surfaced drive provides a smashing walk along to the water gardens, regarded, once again, as the finest in the country. Since the Trust's acquisition of the estate in the early 1980s, these superb gardens have enjoyed an extensive restoration programme, and once again resemble the beautiful scene created throughout the 1700s by the new owners, the Aislabie family. All the buildings such as the temples and the Octagon Tower were also added during this period.

The Temple of Piety across the Moon Pond

Beyond a bend above Half Moon Pond, running above the canalised Skell we are treated to views over the Moon Pond, flanked by crescents with lead statues in attendance, to the Temple of Piety. At the eastern end of the grounds another shop, cafe and toilets see us out to emerge at the lake in Studley Royal deer park. The most direct route omits St. Mary's church and follows the lower pathway by the lake, then towards the end bears left on the road rising to the main avenue. Look back to see the church before turning right on the main route, with Ripon Cathedral in view ahead. To visit the church on entering the deer park, turn immediately left to climb by a car park and up through parkland to the waiting spire.

The direct line of the Way turns up the lane briefly, then bears right along a bridle-track. An access road to the Fountains Abbey Visitor Centre is crossed and the bridleway is preserved on a parallel course. It meets the main access road just past the visitor centre. After crossing the road a path doubles back to the centre, which features information and refreshments. **The bridle-track forges on, soon nearing the access road again. Here a tall gate sees a public footpath into the Studley Royal deer park. The park is entered alongside a tall obelisk, with St. Mary's church just beyond.** St Mary's was completed in 1878, boasting superb stained glass and an impressive great spire prominent in many views around the neighbourhood. It is open on afternoons at Easter and from May to September.

From the church simply advance along the surfaced estate drive, passing the grandiose estate office. Ahead, symbolically, the great limestone walls of Ripon Cathedral soar skywards, often glowing in the lowering sun. After a good stride on the long driveway, look back to see St. Mary's church framed exquisitely beyond the long avenue of limes, laid out to look to the similarly framed cathedral. Now in the heart of this centuries-old deer park, many of these creatures can be discerned, the three breeds present being Red deer, Fallow deer (most numerous) and Sika deer, introduced from Manchuria in the 1600s.

Fallow Deer

Approaching a lodge at the East Entrance arch to the park, either stay on this to the road then go left into Studley Roger, or keep an eye out for a path bearing off left. This rises gently and crosses to a gate in the estate wall. A path heads away with a fence and becomes enclosed at a kissing-gate to drop down onto the road in the village. This unassuming little spot has some attractive cottages featuring red pantile roofs.

Cross straight over past a Victorian postbox and along a short rough road. From a kissing-gate at the end a path heads off into the fields. A fence-side leads the path on through the centre of a large crop field. At a junction with a bridleway, turn sharp right on this path to

approach a house at the end of a plantation. The path becomes enclosed as it is sent around the front of the garden, over a stream. On leaving, note the Studley avenue briefly returning on the right, still leading faithfully to St. Mary's spire. **Resume along the enclosed way to drop to a footbridge and ford at Hell Wath on the river Skell. Just up the other side is a road end at Hellwath Cottage.** Note the substantial limestone wall of Masterman Crag to its right, looking curiously out of place. **Just before the house turn left on a footpath into the trees.** This is Hell Wath Nature Reserve, its grassland supports wild flowers, ash woodland and hawthorn scrub.

A firm path heads through the trees and undergrowth to emerge into open surrounds. Keep left at a couple of forks and the path soon joins the riverbank. This is traced downstream into denser woodland. The unassuming Navigation Stone is passed, commemorating the construction of a canal here in 1820. **A flight of steps lead down to a path junction on the very bank. Keep straight on to a footbridge.** It is worth using the bridge to appraise the confluence of the Skell and the Laver. Of equal girth, the Laver drains the rolling moorlands above Kirkby Malzeard. Fresh from its triumphal journey through Fountains and Studley Park, the Skell gratefully accepts this major bolstering before entering the Cathedral city, though it is to lose its own identity immediately beyond, in the much grander Ure, river of Wensleydale.

The route resumes downstream, and the head of Borrage Green Lane is met to lead out onto the edge of town. The recommended conclusion is as follows: *italicised* features of interest en route are mentioned overleaf. Enter the public area on the left to resume downstream, the path cleverly passing under the road bridge in the company of the river. At the other side it is briefly forced up onto the road, bizarrely named Barefoot Street. An urban footway quickly takes over and leads along the riverbank to *Bondgate Bridge*.

Cross the road to the old church of St. John the Baptist and continue downstream the last couple of minutes to New Bridge at Bondgate Green, climbing steps onto it then crossing the bridge. Take the first turning right along *High St. Agnesgate*. Take the first left at *Cathedral Hall* and up steps beneath an arch to finish in style, at the very walls of *Ripon Cathedral*. For a more secular conclusion, cross the road outside the main door (to the left) and walk along Kirkgate to enter the *Market Square*, where the obelisk makes a fitting finishing point. So does the wide selection of public houses!

• ***RIPON***

Features passed en route to the finish of the walk include:

Bondgate Bridge: This functional structure dates only from 1892, but alongside stands a superb old church on an ancient foundation of AD 1109, originally the Hospital and Chapel of St. John the Baptist.

High St. Agnesgate: On the right is Thorp Prebend House where James I is said to have stayed. Just past it is a surviving Norman arch of the chapel of St. Anne's Hospital, an early almshouse. It stands in front of some red-brick 19th century almshouses.

Cathedral Hall: This stands on the site of a medieval school which became the Free Grammar School of Queen Mary by charter in 1555. On the left in Minster Close is the red-brick Old Hall of 1738 on the site of a medieval Prebendal House. It served as a Canon's Residence in the mid-19th century, during which time the Rev. Charles Dodgson (better known as the author Lewis Carroll) was an annual visitor.

Ripon Cathedral: The Cathedral Church of St. Peter and St. Wilfrid is the third building on the 7th century site of Wilfrid's original monastery, then in the mighty kingdom of Northumbria. Though the church was destroyed by the Danes in the 9th century, the Saxon crypt of 672 AD survives to this day. The present Cathedral dates from the latter half of the 12th century, with various additions down the years, most notably after the partial collapse of the central tower in 1450. Externally it is the imposing West front that draws attention, a stunning high wall filling the end of Kirkgate. Inside there are countless features to admire, including the superb East window and a medieval screen.

Market Square: This is the buzzing heart of Ripon, and each Thursday the market presents a colourful and animated scene. Centrepiece is the 90ft tall obelisk, whose slender lines replaced an earlier Market Cross in 1702. Finest building overlooking the square is the Town Hall of 1801, originally a town house for the owner of Studley Royal. Just doors away is the Wakeman's House with its Tudor facade.

For many centuries Ripon was under ecclesiastical rule known as 'The Liberty', with the Archbishop of York's authority being greater than that of the King. Under this arrangement a 'Wakeman' was responsible for the townsfolk's safety during the hours of darkness, and this setting of the watch was heralded by the sounding of a horn at each corner of the Market Cross. If, therefore, you break off from your Trans-Pennine Way celebrations, then at 9pm you can witness the Wakeman blowing his horn beneath the obelisk to maintain a tradition unbroken for more than a millennium.

Ripon Cathedral from the south

Ripon is the smallest of the seven cities of Yorkshire, the others being Leeds, Sheffield, Bradford, York, Hull and Wakefield. Of numerous other claims to fame, Ripon is the most northerly place to be connected to England's network of navigable waterways. Little more than two miles in length, the Ripon Canal is linked to the river Ure east of the city, and restoration work around the canal basin has breathed new life into the waterway. Ripon also boasts one of the many racecourses in Yorkshire, a local tradition for around 300 years.

Many of the central street names are still 'gates', and the general layout has changed little since medieval times. Indeed, apart from the inevitable addition of modern suburbs, Ripon's greatest change came as recently as 1996, when rumbling waggons bound for the A1 were finally diverted from its congested streets onto a new by-pass. To finish, Ripon also boasts two rather novel museums, both suitably sited in their original gaunt Victorian surroundings: one is the old workhouse, and the other a prison!

A LOG OF THE WALK

Date	Place	Miles stage	Miles total	Notes
	Garstang	-	-	
	Lancaster Canal (end)	2¼	2¼	
	Claughton	4¼	4¼	
	Beacon Fell	7½	7½	
	Chipping	12	12	
	Longridge Fell	3¼	15¼	
	Hurst Green	6½	18½	
	Great Mitton	10¾	22¾	
	Clitheroe	14	26	
	Pendleton	1½	27½	
	Deerstones	4	30	
	Barley	6½	32½	
	A682, Admergill	10	36	
	Salterforth	12¾	38¾	
	Earby	15	41	
	Pinhaw	2½	43½	
	Lothersdale	4¼	45¼	
	Cowling	6½	47½	
	Slippery Ford	9½	50½	
	Hare Hill	12½	53½	
	Haworth	14	55	
	A629, Manywells	3	58	
	B6144, Hewenden	4¼	59¼	
	Harden	5¾	60¾	
	Bingley	8	63	
	Micklethwaite	9½	64½	
	Ilkley	14½	69½	
	Primrose Hill	1¾	71¼	
	A59, Kexgill	5¼	74¾	
	Thruscross	9½	79	
	Yorke's Folly	14½	84	
	Pateley Bridge	16	85½	
	B6265, Blazefield	1¼	86¾	
	Brimham Rocks	4	89½	
	Sawley	8¾	94¼	
	Fountains Abbey	10¾	96¼	
	Ripon	14½	**100**	

SOME USEFUL ADDRESSES

Ramblers' Association 1/5 Wandsworth Road, London SW8 2XX
Tel. 0171-339 8500

Lancashire Countryside Service
Environment Directorate, Winckley House, Cross Street, Preston PR1 8RD
Tel. 01772-264709

Bradford Countryside Service
Rights of Way, Goulbourne Street, Keighley BD21 1JR Tel. 01535-618317

North Yorkshire County Council Public Rights of Way,
Area 3 District, Croft House, Carleton Road, Skipton BD23 2BG
Tel. 01756-793344

The National Trust Yorkshire Region
Goddards, 27 Tadcaster Road, York YO2 2QG Tel. 01904-702021

Youth Hostels Association
Trevelyan House, 8 St. Stephen's Hill, St. Albans AL1 2DY Tel. 01727-845047

Bowland Camping Barns
16 Shawbridge Street, Clitheroe BB7 1LY Tel. 01200-428366

Information Centres
The Bus Station **Preston*** Tel. 01772-556618
The Discovery Centre, High Street **Garstang** Tel. 01995-602125
Bowland Visitor Centre **Beacon Fell** Tel. 01995-640557
12-14 Market Place **Clitheroe*** Tel. 01200-425566 (TIC); 442226 (transport)
Car Park **Barley**
The Bus Station, Broadway **Nelson*** Tel. 01282-698533
Pendle Heritage Centre, Park Hill **Barrowford** Tel. 01282-695366
The Council Shop, Post Office Buildings, Fernlea Avenue **Barnoldswick**
Tel. 01282-666704
9 Sheep Street **Skipton** Tel. 01756-792809
2-4 West Lane **Haworth** Tel. 01535-642329
Station Road **Ilkley** Tel. 01943-602319
14 High Street **Pateley Bridge** Tel. 01423-711147
Royal Baths Assembly Rooms, Crescent Road **Harrogate** Tel.01423-537300
Minster Road **Ripon** Tel. 01765-604625

Public Transport Information
Lancashire: County Information Centres (* in above list)

Metro (West Yorkshire): Tel. 0113-245 7676

North Yorkshire: Tel. 01609-780780

National Rail Enquiries: Tel. 0345-484950

INDEX

Principal features